A CELEBRATION
of
ENGLISH WINE

A CELEBRATION
of
ENGLISH WINE

Liz Sagues

FOREWORD BY OZ CLARKE

ROBERT HALE

First published in 2018 by
Robert Hale, an imprint of
The Crowood Press Ltd
Ramsbury, Marlborough
Wiltshire SN8 2HR

www.crowood.com

British Library Cataloguing-in-Publication Data
A catalogue record for this book is available from the British Library.

ISBN 978 0 7198 2614 6

Front cover image: Chris Dixon Photography/Hambledon Vineyard
Back cover images (from left): The Electric Eye Photography/Hattingley Valley,
Hambledon Vineyard, Albourne Estate
Frontispiece: Nutbourne Vineyards

Typeset by Servis Filmsetting Ltd, Stockport, Cheshire
Printed and bound in India by Replika Press Pvt Ltd

CONTENTS

FOREWORD

THE FIRST ENGLISH VINEYARD I VISITED WAS Staple St James, whose wind-swept acres sprawled above Wingham on the Canterbury to Sandwich road. My mum took me there to meet a wonderfully bucolic, rubicund fellow called Bill Ash, who made bone-dry whites whose prickly, hedgerow scents, seasoned by the salty whip of the northerly gales sweeping up from Richborough, I can still taste today. I don't remember the sun shining much at Staple. I don't remember it being warm at all. And I'm not sure that the vines are there any more. But I remember proud Bill in his lumberjack's shirt, arms akimbo, gazing out over his struggling vines as the breezes flapped at his ruddy pink cheeks. I hope he knew what important work he was doing. Because his dry huxelrebe had as much a sense of place and person and pride as any wine out of France.

And when I became a wine pro – well, I struck lucky again. I clambered and clattered and slithered and stumbled my way down to a hidden eyrie, a tiny golden spot of fairy magic in a fold of the Sussex South Downs. Breaky Bottom. Probably the most beautiful vineyard in Britain. So delicate, so fragile, so precious and held in the loving, caressing bulldog hands of Peter Hall. You learn more about wines, and vineyards, and life – yours, his, what life has been, what life could be – by an expedition to this tiny paradise than you will from any other vineyard in the land.

And this is the greatest joy of Liz Sagues's new book. Whereas I, despite my tremendous enthusiasm for the vineyards that increasingly fan out across our lovely England and Wales, simply haven't visited anything like enough, Liz has. And her book shows it. From the very first chapter she isn't merely giving you the dry facts of vineyards, their history and their wine. Every chapter is imbued with a sense of the people, a sense of the places – the fields, the rocks, the cliffs and glades; the wispy mist, the sleeting rain, the pale, brave sunshine – all of those things that give English wine its unique character. Through her, I can feel the damp and the dry. I can sense the canny, the clever and the callow, and, as I read her words, I can taste the truly original flavours that only our vineyards and our winegrowers can create.

Let me take a couple of sections. The one on 'grapes'. With the current rush to plant the classic champagne varieties, this could be a paean to pinot noir and chardonnay, with the other less fashionable grape varieties trailing muddily behind at a respectful distance. But no. In we dive with two of the most important of Britain's grapes – bacchus and seyval blanc. It's fascinating to read that Norfolk, of all places, with its cooler summers, but drier, sunnier autumns, may provide the perfect site for bacchus. It's a delight to get caught up in the arguments about seyval blanc, one of Britain's most controversial varieties. Owen Elias, for ten years chief winemaker at Chapel Down, the UK's biggest producer, calls seyval 'hideous', while Peter Hall at Breaky Bottom delights in his seyval as 'elegant, sweet-natured'. And their supporters are fairly evenly divided.

Well, if you want to know more about such people, such grape varieties, and what wines they really produce, at the heart of the book is a memorable run of virtual visits to the vineyards. But Liz isn't just telling you about soil and sunshine, crop levels and canopy management. 'People make wine,' she states bluntly, for better or worse. 'The final liquid reflects most of all the individual personality of the person who makes it.' The fact that Liz starts with Peter Hall at Breaky Bottom, goes on to the Lindo family at Camel Valley in Cornwall, and continues with three fascinatingly different views of the possibilities, the pleasures and the perils of organic grape-growing and winemaking in these isles, shows her as a true enthusiast. But she is also an honest critic and a doughty digger after all the myriad of details, opinions and emotions that churn together at the heart of our English wine revolution.

Oz Clarke

Oz Clarke at the presentation of the inaugural UK Wine Awards in July 2017. He and Susie Barrie (in background) co-chaired the judging panel. TOM GOLD PHOTOGRAPHY/WINEGB

ACKNOWLEDGEMENTS

I'M GREATLY INDEBTED TO THE VERY LARGE NUMBER of people who have generously shared information, arranged meetings, guided me through vineyards, answered questions, opened bottles, provided photographs and generally done so much towards the comprehensiveness of this book. If there are errors, they are mine, not theirs. I haven't repeated here the names of those people who are quoted or referred to in the pages that follow – the words there will, I hope, make clear how much they have contributed. But I want to acknowledge the help of a number whose names do not appear: Jo Alcott, Alison Barclay, Rosamund Barton, Céline Bouteiller, Fiona Campbell, Charlotte Dawber, Olivia Drake, Millie Driver, Steffan Griffiths, Astrid Lewis, Anne Linder, Georgia Mallinson, Steven Morris, Katharine O'Callaghan, Sue Olford, Jean Sagues, Jeannette Simpson, Dominic Strange.

A number of illustrations have been sourced through Wikimedia Commons; these are images existing in the public domain or made available under Creative Commons attribution-only licence CC BY 4.0 (http://creativecommons.org/licenses/by-sa/4.0). Specifically, these are: Chapter 1, Samuel Pepys, John Rose, Castell Coch (by Hchc2009, own work); Chapter 4, phylloxera cartoon, wild grape (Bill Summers @ USDA-NRCS PLANTS Database / USDA SCS. 1991. Southern wetland flora: Field office guide to plant species. South National Technical Center, Fort Worth), vine mildew; and Chapter 5, John Evelyn. The British Library and the Wellcome Library (Wellcome Images) have also been much-appreciated sources of free-of-copyright images.

INTRODUCTION

THIS BOOK IS A CELEBRATION IN A DOUBLE SENSE. First, it proclaims the quality level that English – or, to be more geographically correct, UK – wine has reached as the second decade of the twenty-first century draws towards its close. And second, it delights in how very celebratory that wine itself so often is.

Confirmation comes from the very top, from Buckingham Palace and the Houses of Parliament. English is frequently the fizz of choice served to foreign heads of state or at significant royal occasions (think banquet for the Chinese president or Queen Elizabeth II's Jubilee garden party, for example), and increasingly English sparkling wine is replacing champagne in the

The first vine planting in England by a champagne house, at Domaine Evremond in Kent, April 2017.
THOMAS ALEXANDER PHOTOGRAPHY/DOMAINE EVREMOND

cellars of Westminster. Half the wines served at government events now are English or Welsh. Cynics might argue this is simply 'little Britain' patriotism, but the wider world disagrees. Crucially, other nations are now buying English wine, as export sales become a significant entry on the balance sheets of the bigger players.

Then consider professional opinion. There hasn't been one uniquely memorable sparkling wine event to equal the Judgement of Paris, when, in an iconic blind tasting in 1976, red and white wines from California wowed top tasters more than the finest from Bordeaux and Burgundy. But time and again in blind tasting contests against top cuvées of champagne, English sparklers have shone, beating the likes of Pol Roger and Bollinger. The first time that happened there was shock and astonishment. Today, such victories hardly merit a mention, even in the wine trade press.

Quality is obviously crucial, as the many significant international verdicts prove. But quantity is important too if a previously little-considered country is to become a significant part of the wine world. UK vineyard area more than doubled in the decade to 2018, to reach some 2,330 hectares. It is set to go on soaring, and more and more of the plantings are by large, commercially savvy growers. Beyond that, English wine generates news, and not only in trade circles. For example, when confirmation came of the first purchase of vineyard land in

England by a French champagne house (Taittinger's Domaine Evremond, in December 2015), mainstream media attention was intense.

How and why has all this happened? In the pages that follow, I'll attempt to provide some answers. Generally, though, what is most important to realize is that, as the twenty-first century has progressed, a raft of disparate elements have come together to create more change than in the entire previous history of wine grape-growing in the British Isles. A warming climate is allowing grapes to ripen better, even if the British weather remains worryingly unreliable and vineyard yields are still often too low for commercial comfort. An ever-better understanding of the best sites to choose for vineyards and the most appropriate grape varieties to plant on them is now recognized as vital. The professionalism of many of the newcomers, and their openness to bringing in not merely advice but also physical help from people and places beyond Britain, represent a strong and successful contrast to the insular cottage industry approach that used to be too common.

All this doesn't come cheap, and price remains an issue for some potential consumers. While the average retail price of a bottle of wine in the UK hovers below £6, few home-produced still wines are sold for less than £12 – for all but the longest-established producers, it simply isn't possible to cover costs, let alone make

Freshly pressed grape juice at Gusbourne winery in Kent. GUSBOURNE

a profit, below that figure. The sales battle must be won on quality, not price, and there is an increasing realization that the international competition against which English wines should be measured is not supermarket chardonnay from Chile or bland pinot grigio from Italy. Instead, they need to challenge sancerre or chablis or New Zealand sauvignon blanc. And, of course, champagne.

Wine produced in these islands has a history that stretches back to the Romans, continuing through the intervening centuries to the late-twentieth-century pioneers of champagne-style sparkling wine. That will be covered in more detail further on. But what is being poured into glasses today is entirely modern, the product of the enormous progress of the last two decades. English wine was, within my own quite recent vinous memory, in no way a serious proposition in world terms. How different that is now!

As the story is told, there is an issue with words. While this book's title of 'English wine' is an oversimplification of the current, rather wider geographical spread, I make no excuse for using the compression frequently, for both convenience and ease of reading. Beyond England itself there are significant vineyards in Wales, and wine has been made commercially in the Channel Islands since the 1970s. The wetter, colder UK fringes of Northern Ireland and Scotland are not yet proving friendly to intending wine grape-growers, but that may change not too far into the future. So when you read 'English', remember please to be geographically broader-minded.

That leads on to another difficulty: more precise naming of 'English' wine is an on-going issue. The UK vine-growing area in total is only a fraction the size of Burgundy, for example, or the Barossa Valley, yet there are big differences within it, in the base rock and soils, the weather, the grapes grown and the styles of wine produced. Regional identification is valuable, but go too far down that route, with names such as Devonshire or Yorkshire, and there will be only a handful of bottles bearing the label.

And what distinctive identification should the fizz bottles carry? 'English Sparkling Wine' is a clumsy

England's £100 sparkler: Kit's Coty Coeur de Cuvée, made by Chapel Down. CHAPEL DOWN

mouthful, but suggested alternatives have mostly lacked zing or immediately recognizable appeal, and none has yet found universal support. Finding a way to differentiate the UK offering clearly and memorably, without diluting the overall message, is a challenge that is unlikely to be fully solved for many vintages to come.

UK wine must be made from freshly picked, home-grown grapes. RATHFINNY WINE ESTATE

A common confusion must also be avoided. There is English wine and Welsh wine; maybe soon there will be Northern Irish wine and Scottish wine. The rules insist they should all be made from freshly picked grapes grown in these islands. Then there is British wine, which is different. It is made from imported grape concentrate that is diluted and fermented, and then adjusted to the desired style, anything from light table wines to fortified sweet ones. This book is not about British wine.

The broad spread of locations from which true wine comes will be obvious on any map plotting UK vineyards. A swathe of southern England, especially

the chalk and greensand belt that runs through Kent, Sussex and Hampshire, is the heartland of English wine production and this book will, necessarily, focus on that area. But the journey will extend much further north and west – for example, to visit the vineyard that put Cornwall on the international wine map, to meet the family whose grape-growing became a Staffordshire extension of their Punjabi farming heritage, and to understand why vines in Yorkshire escaped the frost that ravaged southern England's vineyards in spring 2017. And that brings me to a third aspect of English wine that is celebrated in this book: the people who have made this drinking pleasure possible, from the anonymous Roman vignerons in Northamptonshire to the twenty-first-century creators of world-beating bubbles.

Before we start the tour, before we meet some of those special people, there is one important point to make. It is easy to get too technical or adjectivally incontinent about wine and I will try to avoid both. Though I did know someone who enjoyed reading the scores of modern music much more than listening to the pieces themselves, so perhaps there are people who take more pleasure in discussing vine clones and soil profiles than in consuming the final liquid.

Wine is for pleasure, for drinking in good company. To increase that pleasure, a deeper understanding often helps and that is particularly true for English wine. It is different, if not as starkly so as it once was. There can be unfamiliar scents and flavours, a green and grassy character that is appealing in good wines but tooth-achingly sharp when the acidity from grapes short of sunshine isn't controlled in the winery. Most importantly, while many differences are down to grape variety and weather, the character of individual wines is also influenced by place and people, by work in the vineyard and winery practice, and by much more

Nyetimber's Tillington vineyard in Sussex, looking towards the South Downs. NYETIMBER

besides. Such factors will be considered in more detail in the chapters to come (this isn't a novel, so you can choose the order in which you read them). One appetiser: as far as weather is concerned, global warming is far from guaranteed good news – it brings more extremes of wind and rain alongside those slightly higher temperatures, and ripening grapes don't like violence. It takes courage and a very deep pocket to be so obsessed with quality, as one leading sparkling wine producer was in the dreary October of 2012, to leave the grapes unpicked in a year when spring, summer and autumn conspired together against the crop. Few can afford such a decision, but the wise know they will most probably face two dreadful years in every decade.

Who knows what developments may have taken place by the time this book is on sale? Some of what is recounted here may have been already overtaken by changing events, or might be soon. But it will still be relevant to a fascinating and fast-moving story. English wine is on an exhilarating and very rapid rollercoaster ride and there will, inevitably, be downs as well as ups as the twenty-first century moves on. But most passengers with it on that rollercoaster – both wine producers and wine drinkers – should remain with broad smiles on their faces.

Chapter 1

The Roots of English Wine Dig Back to Roman Times

Before the Roman came to Rye or out to Severn
strode
The rolling English drunkard made the rolling
English road . . .

G. K. Chesterton's happy evocation of what might be the earliest example of UK wine tourism is one of my favourite poems. Unfortunately for this book, it is far more likely that his early over-imbiber was going in search of ale or cider rather than wine. But wine was certainly known, if not actually made, in Britain before Julius Caesar's tentative incursion in 55 BC. And, with the local product much boosted by imports from often warmer, sunnier locations, it has carried on satisfying UK palates ever since.

There have, not unexpectedly, been hiccups in the home-made supply. The immediate aftermath of Henry VIII's dissolution of the monasteries and the coldest part of the 'little ice age' that soon followed are those most frequently quoted, though not entirely correctly – wine production may have diminished, but it didn't stop in either period. A serious slump came in the nineteenth century, but the real hiatus occurred much more recently, as the two world wars and their repercussions largely put paid to wine grape-growing for three decades. Now, we're in a time of global warming, and with it – though certainly not only because of it – the English wine revival is resplendent.

The earliest vines in British soil

When were grapes first grown for wine in the British Isles? In the absence of firm evidence, it is impossible to be definitive, and the fact that vine pollen dating back some 400,000 years has been found in Essex in no way means that wine was made by Britain's earliest hominids. Worldwide, current evidence points to the first pure grape wine being made far to the east, in Georgia, in the sixth millennium BC, although fermented beverages including grapes but not made solely of them are known to have been made in China a little earlier. Much more realistically, argument continues over whether in the first century AD Tacitus was correct in saying that the vine couldn't flourish in Britain. However, from the latter part of the third century, Britain was one of several Roman provinces where the inhabitants were, by edict of Emperor Probus, specifically permitted to cultivate vineyards and make wine. There is every possibility that they did so, probably even before they were given that formal authorization.

The best evidence comes from the gravel extraction site of Wollaston in the Nene Valley, Northamptonshire, just south of Wellingborough and close to the Roman town of Irchester. Archaeologists worked for five years in the 1990s alongside a 3-kilometre stretch of a major Roman road. They found a large area – 7.5 hectares, appreciably bigger than the average size of a modern English vineyard – where narrow, steep-sided parallel trenches had been cut, filled with topsoil or manure and plants set in them 1.5 metres apart, with stakes for support. Pottery from the trenches suggested a second to third century AD date for the site.

Was it a vineyard? 'There can be little doubt,' reported the excavation team, which was led by Ian Meadows, then head of Northamptonshire Archaeology. Samples of pollen from the trenches and surrounding drainage ditch indicated that vines grew there, alongside grasses and weeds of cultivation. Also,

the widely spaced trenches matched the shape of those in vineyards discovered in other parts of the Roman empire, notably France, and replicated the continental vine-cultivation practice of *pastinatio*, as described by contemporary natural historians. This was, said the Wollaston archaeologists, 'an important indication of Roman agricultural innovation in Britain'.

Overall, Meadows and his colleagues estimated, the vineyard would have covered some 11 hectares; with several other sites identified in the vicinity, this indicated that the Nene Valley was a major wine-producing area. 'Wine produced on this scale would have been a significant cash crop, and it is unlikely that it was entirely consumed locally,' they added, arguing that the discovery implies that wine was far more important in Roman Britain than anyone had previously believed. 'Wine probably never supplanted beer as the "national" drink in Roman Britain, but the new evidence suggests that viticulture may have had a greater impact than previously envisaged.'

Academic accounts in the journal *Antiquity* apart, the findings were also less formally reported in the magazine *Current Archaeology*, under the headline 'Wollaston: The Nene Valley, a British Moselle?' The vineyard, wrote Meadows in that article, 'represented a major capital investment by the original owner(s)'. He continued: 'Over six kilometres of trench were dug

One of the Wollaston vineyard trenches, showing the holes for stakes and vine roots. MUSEUM OF LONDON ARCHAEOLOGY

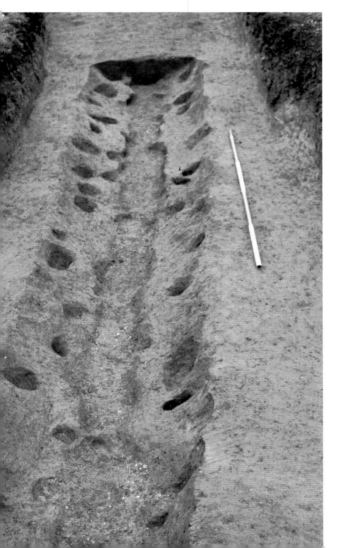

and, on the basis of plant spacing at every 1.5m, there were at least 4000 separate vines. This would allow for the production of about 15,000 bottles of white wine each year.' When he talks to a non-specialist audience, he likens that number of bottles to the volume of liquid carried by a petrol delivery tanker. The comparison helps to indicate the scale of what he emphasizes was 'a major commodity, produced in vast amounts'.

One possible point of concern is that no specific vine-growing tools have been found at the Nene Valley sites. Many of those used, though, would have been common to other types of farming, and Meadows suggests he and his colleagues perhaps 'missed a trick' by concentrating more on them than on considering the containers in which the wine travelled away from its source. These were probably barrels, as no local styles of amphora have been found. Given the fragility of wood, the barrels themselves were unlikely to survive, but what of the tools of the coopers who made them?

Another unknown is where the grapes were processed, although this was possibly done in a nearby villa or at Irchester. And there must have been a market for those thousands of litres of wine, so what is the answer to the most intriguing question of all: who drank it? The enthusiasm for wine in imperial Rome is legendary, with some historians estimating that everyone, from the emperor's entourage to slaves, consumed approximately a bottle a day. Away from their homeland, Roman soldiers were granted a regular allowance of what is generally thought to have been wine, and the banqueting upper classes were happy imbibers, as evidenced from wall paintings in villas in all parts of the empire. Given the scale of production at Wollaston alone, there were surely indigenous British drinkers too. And further evidence suggests that the local supply was by no means sufficient.

An altar, made of Yorkshire millstone grit and dating to AD 237, was found a century ago during excavations in Bordeaux. The inscription identifies its owner, Marcus Aurelius Lunaris, as a high-ranking priest in the Roman colonies of Lincoln and York. He had dedicated the altar to the French city's protective Roman goddess

Tutela Boudiga before he set off from York on what is thought to have been a regular journey across the water. Scholars believe that the wealthy Lunaris was likely to have been a merchant as well as a priest and, given his destination, could well have been involved in the wine trade. Was he alone in that role? Most probably not.

The Nene Valley vine-growing area has recently been confirmed as extending to the north of Wellingborough as well as around Wollaston to the south, but these were not the only vineyards established in Roman Britain. While archaeologists have to take care over interpreting the plentiful finds of grape pips as evidence for the existence of others – most pips more probably came from imported table grapes – vines appear to have been planted in various parts of southern England and as far north as Lincolnshire. Ian Meadows argues that, once the Romano-British farmers had discovered that their vines would grow happily without using the elaborate *pastinatio* system, many more would have planted them. Places where cuttings were pushed directly into the ground, with small stakes to support them, don't register even in sophisticated archaeological surveys, but they surely existed in some profusion. Meadows will continue to be among those aiming to find them. After all, he says, for someone in his profession who enjoys a glass of wine, this is an unusually rewarding research area.

After the Romans, the wine-drinking monks

What happened before the Romans? As I write, earlier evidence of vine cultivation or winemaking has yet to be found in Britain. However, wine was drunk by the Belgic tribes who immediately preceded the Romans in southern and eastern England. Maybe they didn't make their own, but there is little doubt that they imported it: amphorae and even a silver wine cup have been found in high-status graves.

And after the Romans? Despite the ale-swilling preferences of the nordic and germanic invaders, wine was a crucial element in Anglo-Saxon Britain's developing Christian religious culture, among followers of both the

The importance of wine in England's religious communities – though rather later than the Saxon monarchs' vineyard gifts – is shown by these early fourteenth-century English miniatures, from the Queen Mary Psalter and the 'Welles Apocalypse' by Peter of Peckham. BRITISH LIBRARY

local Celtic and the imported Roman rites. Monastic communities existed in various UK locations from the early fifth century onwards, almost immediately after the Romans' departure, and they needed to be self-sufficient in wine as well as food. Hence in 731 Bede noted at the very beginning of his *Ecclesiastical History of England* that the country 'produces vines in some places'. It would be risky indeed to hazard a guess as to what varieties these vines were, and the quality of the drink made from their grapes, but a tradition had been established, which today is manifested in England's world-beating sparkling wines.

Continuing post-Roman viticulture is confirmed, for example, by King Alfred's introduction of a law ordering compensation be paid by any man who damaged another's vine; by the decision of Alfred's great grandson, King Eadwig, to grant a vineyard in Somerset to Glastonbury Abbey; and by another royal donation of a Somerset vineyard, at Watchet, this time from King Edgar to Abingdon Abbey. There is even an argument from eighteenth-century antiquary Joseph Strutt that the Saxons called October the 'Wyn Moneth', to mark the importance of the grape harvest.

Move on to the late eleventh century and Domesday Book, William I's detailed inventory of his newly conquered country, has forty-two definite records of vineyards, more of them owned by aristocrats than by monasteries. Remarkably, there are none listed in what are present-day Hampshire or East or West Sussex, and barely a handful in Kent and Surrey – the counties that today have easily the largest concentration of English vineyards. Was Domesday accurate, or were its surveyors so influenced by the excellence of those counties' liquor that they neglected their recording duties? Whichever, English vineyards multiplied and their product was good: 'The wine has in it no unpleasant tartness or eagerness, and is little inferior to the French in its sweetness,' wrote William of Malmesbury around 1150. Gloucestershire, he contended, was the best county, both for the fertility of the vineyards and the sweetness of their grapes; vines were grown in the open without sheltering walls and were trained up poles. The taste then was clearly for sweet wines.

Royal involvement

English wine was not simply the drink of kings and of many of their subjects. The royals also made it – or at least they owned vineyards. Henry II had established one in the grounds of Windsor Castle by the mid-twelfth century and it flourished, producing more wine than the royal household needed and selling on the excess. The site was still recorded as 'vineyard' on nineteenth-century plans and, happily, that historic link has been revived, with the planting in 2011 of chardonnay, pinot noir and pinot meunier vines in Windsor Great Park. The first vintage of commercial sparkling wine, from 2013, sold out immediately on its release, in September 2016. The Duke of Edinburgh supported the venture, which was the initiative of Tony

STEVEN MORRIS/LAITHWAITE'S WINE

Laithwaite, the man behind the biggest mail-order/online wine club organization in the UK, who just happened to spend his childhood in Windsor and to open his first wine shop in the town.

But didn't English wine largely disappear at the very time Henry planted his vineyard? His wife, Eleanor of Aquitaine, had brought into English royal hands the vast wine-producing lands of Bordeaux. So why, the argument often runs, didn't imports from France meet all the kingdom's needs? It seems not. Was it patriotism, or convenience, or simply that English and French wines appealed to different tastes? Whether for one of these reasons or for some other, vines continued to be planted in English soil, grapes harvested and wine made and drunk in quantity at many levels of society.

All this was clearly commonplace in those post-Conquest centuries, with the production tasks involved illustrated in many surviving sources: manuscript

Present replacement of vines past: the twenty-first-century Windsor Great Park Vineyard. STEVEN MORRIS/LAITHWAITE'S WINE

illustrations, carvings in churches and cathedrals, monastic records and a wealth of other documents. Known vineyards include one planted at Beaulieu Abbey in Hampshire by Cistercian monks in the thirteenth century (vine-growing returned here in the twentieth century); another was a feature in the kitchen garden of a fourteenth-century Bishop of Ely at his London house, in Holborn. In southern England there is hardly a town without at least one 'vine' street name or a county without a cabinetful of records relating to vineyards and local wine production.

Drinking wine, too, was a common – and sometimes over-indulged – pleasure, one not confined to the noble, privileged and religious alone. A number of the fourteenth-century pilgrims in Geoffrey Chaucer's *Canterbury Tales* were serious imbibers: the Summoner 'drank strong blood red wine untill dizzy', while the description of the Franklin noted that 'no man had his cellars better stocked with wine'. Chaucer, whose father and grandfather were vintners, was himself granted a generous daily allowance of wine – a pitcher or a gallon according to which source you choose – by Edward III, whom he served in a variety of roles.

But the poet's Pardoner fulminated against all such indulgence:

A lecherous thing is wine . . .
Oh drunken man, disfigured is your face,
Sour is your breath, foul are you to embrace . . .
Now keep you from the white and from the red.

Modern reproduction of the bird pecking grapes carved on a fourteenth-century misericord at Lincoln Cathedral.
OAKAPPLE DESIGNS LTD

women who drank the medieval English product. The story that follows may be apocryphal, but it's too good not to share. When King John visited the monks at Beaulieu he took one sip of their wine and ordered: 'Send ships forthwith to fetch some good French wine.' That could have indicated the usual standard of monastic wine, or perhaps the royal beaker was filled from a bad vintage – something far from unknown, even in that generally mild time. So much for modern climate change: from the ninth to the late thirteenth centuries, England appears to have had warmer summers, and also more rain, than in the mid-twentieth century.

On, then, to a chillier period for English wine producers – though one caused only partly by a change in the weather. Henry VIII's decision in 1536 to dissolve the monasteries of his kingdom most probably had much less effect on wine grape-growing than many commentators have assumed; after all, the wine-drinking nobles who took over the monastic estates were handed productive vineyards, sparing them the effort and time to establish vines from scratch. Also,

Perhaps he had good reason to preach that message, and not only because of the dangers of intoxication. While the pilgrims' wines, it seems, were often red and maybe imported, pity many of those men and

Men picking grapes on a fourteenth-century misericord in Gloucester Cathedral. WWW.MISERICORDS.CO.UK

many of the senior clerics themselves moved from monasteries to new religious positions in more secular surroundings – and they weren't banned from making their own wine.

But climate did become something of an issue. The 'little ice age', which peaked in the sixteenth and seventeenth centuries, didn't totally stop vines flourishing, but it made producing good wine rather more difficult. Yet in his 1586 history *Britannia*, William Camden offered an alternative reason for the sixteenth-century decline. He blamed the barrenness of once-fruitful land much more on 'the sloth of the inhabitants than the indisposition of the climate'. Hugh Barty-King, a painstaking historian of English wine, supports Camden's argument: 'It seems to me the most sensible observation ever made on English viticulture: it remained as true throughout the following centuries as it was when it was made.' Why? Because, as Barty-King sensibly reasons, while decent wines can be made easily in hotter places, success in borderline climates such as England's requires more work, closer attention to the vines and precise application of broad technical knowledge.

The right places, the right people

The detail of successful modern wine production in England will follow in later chapters, but already in the thirteenth century there was good counsel to be had on the best choice of sites for vineyards. By the end of the sixteenth century and on into the seventeenth, advice on both vineyard location and vine variety was proliferating. Often it was along rather similar lines to that offered hundreds of years later, suggesting planting the same vines as those that flourished along the Rhine or around Paris and siting them on warm, sunny, well-drained hillsides.

Largely, if not uniquely, the growing of vines appears to have been the province of the upper classes; there is a dearth of information on whether lesser mortals copied them. By far the biggest viticultural project in Britain at this time was Lord Salisbury's, at Hatfield House in Hertfordshire. In 1611 20,000 vines were brought there from France, shortly followed by another 10,000. The vineyard flourished for three decades at least. Visiting in 1643, the diarist John Evelyn described the garden and vineyard as 'the most considerable rarity besides the house'. However, things seem to have gone somewhat awry for a while subsequently; in 1661, Samuel Pepys took an after-dinner stroll at Hatfield: 'I walked all alone to the Vineyard which is now a very beautiful place again.' Neither writer mentioned the Hatfield House wine. Pepys did have a happy experience of English wine when in 1667 he visited Admiral Sir William Batten: 'And there, for joy, he did give the company . . . a bottle or two of his own last year's wine, growing at Walthamstow.' The guests' verdict was that it was better than any foreign wine they had encountered.

Evelyn had a rather closer involvement with seventeenth-century English wine, despite his dismissal of one example he encountered as 'good for little'. After meeting John Rose, gardener to King Charles II, and talking to him at length about vines, the diarist was persuaded to write the preface to Rose's *The English Vineyard Vindicated*, published in 1666. (Three years later it was combined in a single binding with

Samuel Pepys, by John Hayls.

John Rose presents a pineapple to his employer, King Charles II, by Thomas Stewart.

Evelyn's translation into English of a more general horticultural work, *The French Gardiner*; included too was Evelyn's own detailed account of winemaking, *The Vintage*.) Rose dedicated his short work to his employer, declaring that he knew that the king 'can have no great opinion of our English Wines'. But their defects were due neither to the climate nor to the work-shy attitude of those who tended the vines, he insisted. Follow his directions on choice of soil and situation, grape variety and cultivation practice, and 'that precious liquor may haply once againe recover its just estimation'.

In 1670 another gardener to nobility, Will Hughes, expanded his advice to would-be vine-growers in an enlarged edition of his work *The Compleat Vineyard: or,*

An Excellent way for the Planting of Vines, According to the German & French manner, and long practised in England. Hughes, too, argued that 'excellent good wine' could be produced in England. Like John Rose, both he and Samuel Hartlib, another advocate of the potential of English wine, whose *The Compleat Husband-man* had been published in 1659, set down specific rules on vineyard site location and named the best grape varieties for successful cultivation. Hartlib and Hughes favoured the Rhenish-grape and the parsley vine (the latter more for show and rarity than profit, commented Hughes); Hartlib also recommended the Paris-grape and the small muskadell, while on Hughes's list came the frantinick and three varieties of muscadine, two white and a red; Rose suggested considerably more varieties.

For much of this historical information I'm indebted to Hugh Barty-King, a prolific writer on a myriad of subjects whose research skills were indefatigable. His *A Tradition of English Wine* was published in 1977, but there is one chapter, 'Viticulture Becomes Scientific and Commercial', that comes remarkably close to describing the situation today – except that it recounts what happened in the years 1700 to 1800. Time and again in those thirty-four pages appear arguments that current supporters of the home-grown product still too often have to refute: that making wine in England is an eccentric activity; that English wine has little appeal for many drinkers; that growing vines 'to any tolerable perfection' is 'altogether impracticable'; that drinkers lack the enthusiasm to try something different; that to sell English wine its origin must be hidden from potential buyers until they have tasted it. Some of the eighteenth-century facts anticipate the present, too: that even the wealthiest estate owners can find costs so high they need to seek loans to continue producing wine; that some English estates employ French winemakers, or the sons (and now daughters too) of English estate owners go to France to learn viticultural skills; that successful producers play a valuable role in promoting their country. Certainly, there were challenges, but increasingly palatable wine was being made.

Growth on a larger scale

The upshot of the emphasis on more professional wine grape-growing in the eighteenth century was that large vineyards were successfully established. One was close to Godalming in Surrey, on the Westbrook estate of James Oglethorpe, MP for Haslemere, where two long south-facing terraces were constructed and planted with vines in the 1720s. Oglethorpe's hospitality was renowned; his wine flowed generously at the many soirées and political gatherings he organized, and his guests feasted on snails fattened on the leaves of his vines. The vineyard survived for a hundred years, still mentioned in 1823 in sale particulars for the estate.

Charles Hamilton shortly before he began his Painshill Park venture, by Antonio David. PAINSHILL PARK TRUST

A little shorter-lived but better known was another initiative in Surrey, near Cobham, close to today's junction of the M25 and the A3. In 1738 the Honourable Charles Hamilton, youngest son of the Duke of Abercorn, began leasing land on the Painshill estate, and set to work transforming it into an extravagant 120-hectare private pleasure ground, enhanced by a multitude of follies. But the vineyard he created on a south-facing slope rolling down to a large artificial lake was no romantic fancy. It was a serious project.

In 1748 Hamilton employed a French vigneron to care for his vines and oversee the whole estate. There was a problem, however. The recruit, David Geneste, came from a family who had grown grapes in Bordeaux for generations, but, after a good number of years as a refugee in England (he was a Huguenot), he had forgotten much of what he had learned as a boy. His solution was an appeal to his sister, still in France, which brought the information he needed and also essential tools, and the vineyard flourished.

The first Painshill wines were reds, but they were harsh and unfit to drink, so Hamilton turned to white and 'to my great amazement my wine had a finer flavour than the best champaign I ever tasted'. More than simply having the flavour of champagne, the two wines – one clear white, the other a delicate bronze pink – also bubbled. 'Both of them sparkled and creamed in the glass,' said a contemporary report repeating their maker's words. How Hamilton achieved that effect is not recorded, but by the mid-1750s the selection of vines at Painshill had grown to include varieties originating from Burgundy – the tender auvergnat, possibly related to pinot noir, and the hardier miller, often identified now as pinot meunier. These could perhaps have been ancestors of the grapes that go into today's English sparkling wine. But no fuss was made about the origin of the wine. Hamilton was well aware of the prejudice towards 'any thing of English growth' and deemed it 'most prudent not to declare' where his wine came from until it had been tasted and approved.

That strategy worked. In a letter to his sister, David Geneste wrote that his employer was selling the excellent white wine from the 1753 harvest for sixty guineas (£63) a barrel, and local customers bought Painshill wines at half a guinea (52.5p) a bottle. However, despite the respect the wine gained and the income it produced, Hamilton's extravagant park emptied even its wealthy creator's deep pockets. He failed to meet interest payments on a loan and in 1773 was forced to sell.

Hamilton's legacy was important, as Barty-King acknowledges: 'Thrice married, he was one of the most colourful men of his time and certainly the most enterprising viticulturist.' He had set new standards that others were to follow. And in happy remembrance of the park's former owner, the charitable Painshill Park Trust in 1992–93 replanted the vineyard, albeit at half its original size, as part of its overall restoration of the estate.

The prejudice against English wine – and an increasing concentration on glasshouse-grown table grapes – failed to halt its production. While it seems that figures for the quantities produced at Westbrook and Painshill have not survived, there was certainly more wine than the gentlemen growers needed, with the surplus finding a market in the inns of surrounding Surrey villages. These vineyards may well have been the biggest yet in Britain, but there are records of plenty more eighteenth-century locations around London, in Kent, Hampshire, the West Country, East Anglia and even Shropshire where vines were grown. A particularly large one on the edge of Bath produced 66 hogsheads in good years, if the figure quoted by Hugh Barty-King is to be believed. In twenty-first-century terms, that equates to close to 13,500 litres or nearly 18,000 modern-day bottles – a huge figure. (Converting historic measures for modern comparison is a numerical mine-field, so I've used the commonest estimates: before 1824 a hogshead of wine held 43 to 46 imperial gallons and after that date the volume was 52.5.)

Even more impressive, according to Barty-King – whose 'reliable' source was again H.M. Tod's *Vine-growing in England* (1911) – was the 60-pipe yield in 1763 of a vineyard established by the tenth Duke of Norfolk at Arundel Castle in Sussex. A pipe had twice the capacity of a hogshead, so the duke's wine could have filled around 32,000 75-centilitre bottles. Yet contemporary plans indicate that his vineyard covered barely a hectare, and there were no others in the castle grounds. Something must be wrong here, for so much wine to come from so small an area. Present-day English yields from a hectare of vineyard are far, far lower, averaging around 2,700 bottles. They surely wouldn't have been almost twelve times that in the eighteenth century.

A little more investigation indicates that there seems to have been a misinterpretation of the original information, which can be traced back to a weighty collection of papers on agriculture, commerce, arts and manufactures entitled *Museum rusticum et commerciale* and published from 1764 onwards by the Society for the Encouragement of Arts, Manufacturers & Commerce. What was reported there, according to two accounts

Painshill Park, folly and vineyard, now restored. AUTHOR

published not long afterwards, puts a subtly different slant on the matter. The duke's cellar was referred to as *containing* (my emphasis) in 1763 'sixty pipes of excellent Burgundy, the produce of a vineyard attached to the castle'. Arundel Castle wine, but more likely the product of many years' harvests, not of a single one.

The duty argument: should French wine face a high import levy?

Statistics apart, the cross-Channel quality comparison is appropriate. English wine needed to be as good as Burgundy's, because, as the nineteenth century dawned and Napoleon blockaded Britain, the French product became much harder to obtain and increasingly expensive. This was a time of much yo-yoing of import duty on wine, French in particular, with an inevitable impact on the popularity of home-produced bottles. In 1787 Prime Minister William Pitt the Younger, clearly not a fan of English wine, had halved the import duty per gallon (450 centilitres approximately, or six bottles) from eight shillings (40p) to four shillings. By encouraging French imports, that reduction would, he told the House of Commons, 'supplant only an useless and pernicious manufacture in this country'. Sure enough, sales of French wine soared.

It didn't take long for the low-duty policy to be reversed. Successive increases more than tripled the levy by 1807, and a further hike in 1813 brought it to only a few pennies less than £1. That last rise was intended to boost, if in only a small way, the British government's wartime finances. It also helped the home vine-growers, as Benjamin Oliveira, MP for Pontefract and a determined opponent of oppressive wine import duties, told the Commons in 1856: 'The British wine trade has grown up in a comparatively short period, in consequence of the prohibitory duty upon foreign wines, and is at this present time a very thriving and increasing branch of commerce.'

Although the duty had decreased from the 1813 peak, even at the then-current 5s 9d, he argued, a reduction would encourage wine drinking at the expense of spirit drinking and the 'crime and misery' linked to the latter. It would also bring an overall higher revenue, an argument that continues to be made today as the wine trade in the UK rails against the present high excise duty levels that apply to both home-produced and imported wine.

Oliveira's failure to bring about change seemingly didn't deter those who were determined to continue drinking fine foreign wine, even if they had to pay more heavily than they wished for their claret. Yet there were others who argued the local case – that it was an Englishman's patriotic duty to produce his own wine and that he could make a very decent one, perhaps one even more palatable than those pricey imports. Once again, the lessons learned from earlier centuries had to be drummed into the heads of those who had land to plant and money to invest, to revive a broad enthusiasm for English wine. And, tellingly, there were the first suggestions of experimenting with imported American vines as a better bet to survive rot and disease.

Just a few took up the challenge of planting on a large scale, with the most ambitious scheme instigated by a Scotsman, on land in Wales. Castell Coch, close to Cardiff, was the location chosen by John Patrick Crichton-Stuart, third Marquess of Bute.

Crichton-Stuart, whose family interest in Cardiff docks and coal made him one of the wealthiest men in Britain, loved all things medieval. He restored both Castell Coch and Cardiff Castle to an elaborated version of their thirteenth-century glories – so why not add a vineyard at the former, to follow the tradition of the nobles and monks of the period? The chosen site beneath the castle walls was actually quite suitable for vines: a protected south-facing slope with limestone bedrock.

After an extended tour of French vineyards at harvest time in 1874, Lord Bute's head gardener, Andrew Pettigrew, returned with two main grape variety recommendations, gamay noir (finally, a grape which is known today!) and miel blanc. The first 2,000 vines were scarcely planted on the 1.2-hectare site before the enterprise was ridiculed on a national scale, most notably in *Punch* magazine. If wine was ever produced from such an unsuitable location, the magazine predicted cynically, it would take four men to drink it – the actual consumer, two others to hold him down and the fourth to force the liquid down his throat.

The early harvests were poor, in quantity at least, the first producing only 240 bottles. But by 1887 – a particularly good year for a place where vintage variation, largely due to poor summers, was extreme – the output had risen to around 3,000 bottles, all white. By the mid-1890s, production of both white and red wine in good vintages reached 12,000 bottles. These are realistic production figures, especially as over its productive lifetime (until the outbreak of the First World War) the original Castell Coch vineyard had been joined by another close by, bringing the area of vines to nearly 5 hectares.

Castell Coch wines were much liked and even proved to be a good investment, substantially increasing in value in buyers' cellars. They were also made available far beyond Wales. In 1897 Lord Bute appointed as his agent London wine merchants Hatch Mansfield, releasing through them eight wines priced from 36 shillings to 48 shillings (£1.80 to £2.40) a dozen bottles. They were described thus on the merchants' list: 'Generally speaking they are soft, sweet, full-bodied, and of a luscious character, very suitable for dessert purposes.'

Castell Coch: below its walls the Marquess of Bute planted his vineyard. CREATIVE COMMONS HCHC2009

These Welsh wines, 'a novelty', had no expense spared in their production, the list continued, and, while they did not yet quite match the finest foreign wines in aroma and flavour, 'they are eminently honest and wholesome'. Their sweetness was due to the addition of sugar before fermentation, a practice essential to achieve wines of decent alcohol level from places where it is difficult to ripen grapes fully; in the case of Castell Coch, a very large quantity of sugar was used.

Hatch Mansfield has continued to flourish since that time, although with a portfolio of non-UK wines. That is now changing, as in 2015 the company joined with Champagne Taittinger to create Domaine Evremond in Kent, the first confirmed purchase of vineyard land in England by a champagne house. Vine planting began in 2017, and hopefully this will prove a more respected and longer-lasting business initiative than the Welsh wines, which were described as 'not exactly a success'.

HATCH, MANSFIELD & CO., LTD. | 1, Cockspur Street, London, S.W.
Quai des Chartrons 68, Bordeaux.

WELSH WINES.

"Canary Brand"

From the MARQUESS OF BUTE'S Vineyards.

➤ A NOVELTY.◄

THESE Wines are the outcome of an experiment initiated some twenty years ago by the Marquess of BUTE on portions of his Estate in Glamorganshire, South Wales.

The cultivation of Vines in Great Britain for the production of Wine is no new thing in the middle ages home-grown Wine was produced of more or less merit, and is frequently referred to in terms of commendation by the Elizabethan writers.

In the present revival of the Industry the best French Vines have been selected after careful trial, and no expense has been spared to attain success, and although the Wines cannot yet be said to possess the delicate aroma and flavour of the best foreign Wines, they are eminently honest and wholesome.

HATCH, MANSFIELD & CO., LTD. | 1, Cockspur Street, London, S.W.
Quai des Chartrons 68, Bordeaux.

WELSH WINES.
"Canary Brand."

Bin No.	Description.	Vintage	Price per doz. bottles
401	Big Soft Wine, Medium Dry	1892	36 -
402	Full Golden Wine, Rather Dry	1891	38/-
403	Rich Full Wine	1890	40/-
404	Full Golden, Rather Sweet ...	1887	44 -
405	Light Golden, Mellow	1887	44/-
406	Dark Golden, Medium Sweet	1887	44 -
407	A Luscious, Golden Wine ...	1887	44 -
408	A Full, Sweet, Brown Wine ...	1885	48 -

Guaranteed by the Marquess of BUTE to be the produce of his Vineyards and to be of the vintage named on the label.

The quantities remaining undisposed of are small; generally speaking they are soft, full bodied, and of a luscious character, very suitable for dessert purposes.

The prices include payment of carriage to any Railway Station in Great Britain, or Port in Ireland.

Sample bottles can be had, Carriage Paid, at the prices quoted on application to

HATCH, MANSFIELD & CO., LTD.,
1, Cockspur Street, Trafalgar Square, S.W.

Three men who launched the boat

This is the right moment to move into almost modern times, skipping over the beginning of the twentieth century. Little more of note happened before the outbreak of the First World War, and from then onwards, until the 1950s, commercial-scale English wine saw its biggest decline since its Roman beginnings. All credit then to the three people who did most to rekindle the flame of interest: horticulturist and pest control expert George Ordish, who had planted a vineyard at Yalding in Kent in 1939; and writer and broadcaster Edward Hyams, in Kent, and research chemist turned enthusiastic gardener Raymond Barrington Brock, in Surrey, with their immediately post-war projects.

Ordish may not have been the most important of the three in terms of his viticultural work, but the reason he became involved is particularly appropriate today. Early in his career he had worked in Champagne, and noticed just how similar the region's climate was to that of his home county. Why were there no vineyards in Kent, he wondered, so he set about creating his own, on a very small scale. Unlike today's successful growers, he didn't choose champagne grape varieties. Instead, he planted a mix of hybrids and crosses, then considered the best for outdoor growing in England but much less favoured now. The wine he made was reasonable, and the knowledge he gained prompted him to write two books on vine-growing in England, plus another on that curse of late nineteenth-century continental winemakers, phylloxera.

Edward Hyams grew grapes for both wine and table, as part of a self-sufficiency project. He and his wife had a large vegetable and fruit garden, even including a plot for tobacco, at their home not far from Ordish's. Their wine needs, noted Hyams, were 'a litre per head per day'! He planted a host of different imported grape varieties, and sought out established old varieties in Kent and further afield.

Much more important than his vine-growing was Hyams' role in spreading the word that good wine could be made in England. Books, articles and broadcasts prompted a great deal of interest in a product that very few people knew about or were able to access. His message reached a huge audience. 'Perhaps ten years hence,' he wrote in the *Daily Mirror* in 1950, 'you'll be raising a glass of sparkling Canterbury in honour of the men who made an English wine industry possible.'

One twenty-first century example of vine planting in Kent, at Simpsons Wine Estate. SIMPSONS WINE ESTATE

Could he have realized how truly prophetic, if a little premature, those words were?

The major grape researcher of this influential trio was Raymond Barrington Brock, whose enthusiasm for

Sparkling Canterbury? SIMPSONS WINE ESTATE

gardening moved from the outdoor growing of peaches to table and wine grapes and a project to identify which varieties would flourish outdoors in England's capricious climate. From 1945, on land around his home high on the North Downs close to Oxted, he attacked his goal with the precision of a dedicated scientist. In one experiment, he planted the same variety of vine against seven different wall surfaces, in order to assess individual performance. His vineyard areas were carefully divided into trial plots, laid out in precise, very closely planted rows and bordered by low-growing fruit trees.

Zealously looking for varieties to plant, Brock appealed first for cuttings from vines already growing in England, then contacted vine research bodies throughout Europe and beyond to grow – literally – his database. The cuttings arrived, directly or indirectly, from likely or unlikely places, among them France,

Switzerland, Belgium, Scandinavia, Russia and various parts of the United States. In return, as his own work began to show results, Brock sent back information and cuttings to his worldwide friends, helping to expand understanding of cool-climate vine-growing on a far wider scale. Among his correspondents was Pierre Galet, then considered the world's greatest expert on vine identification and classification. Galet offered his support for personal as well as professional reasons: he was, he said, English from his mother's family. There were examples of non-plant exchanges, as well – Brock sent pencils and secateurs to ill-equipped Russian researchers in return for wine from two rare Caucasian varieties.

From the first plantings of a dozen varieties in 1946, the scale of work at Brock's Oxted Viticultural Research Station grew and grew. In 1947 twenty-nine varieties were represented in the 1,400 vines; by 1950 those figures had grown respectively to sixty and 7,000-plus. In all, Brock trialled some 600 different grape varieties over 25 years. Among them were the grapes that were soon to become crucial players in the English wine revival – müller-thurgau and seyval blanc. Many others were far less successful, with Brock sometimes despairing of time spent on fruitless work. One batch of recommended French hybrids, he complained, 'all proved hopeless after five years of testing', and some American hybrid cuttings sent to him from New

Müller-thurgau vines growing at Denbies Wine Estate – Ray Barrington Brock introduced the variety to England. AUTHOR

Zealand appear to have ended up in the compost heap without a mention of their quality.

Brock also turned his hand to making wine from his myriad choice of grapes. Initially, things didn't go well, a large part of his first vintage being consigned to a trial in vinegar making and some subsequent efforts ruined by oxidation or mould. But his skills had improved sufficiently by 1960 to encourage him to host a tasting of still and sparkling wines for respected trade guests, many of whom were entitled to put the prized letters of the wine profession's top qualification, Master of Wine, after their names. Reactions were mixed, but Brock didn't seem to mind, arguing that, alongside finding good varieties, he needed to eliminate unsatisfactory ones. He also encouraged visitors to his experimental vineyard, holding open days for the public as well as for wine trade professionals.

Brock subsidized the research station from his own income – he was managing director of a scientific instrument company until 1960 and continued working afterwards – and employed a full-time assistant. He developed his own improvements to the standard treatment for the powdery mildew that attacked his vines, wrote and lectured extensively and even had time for his hobbies of motor racing and car design. A remarkable man indeed, who, before his death in 1999 at the age of ninety-one, witnessed the resurgence of English wine to which he had contributed so much.

The value of the work of these three men is perfectly summed up by the words of Stephen Skelton, in *The Wines of Britain and Ireland* (2001):

> Between them, Ray Brock, Edward Hyams and George Ordish had questioned why it was that outdoor viticulture in the British Isles had all but died out and had, to a certain extent, shown how it might be revived. Although they had not discovered all the answers, they had, through a combination of practical demonstration, scientific research and publicity, generated sufficient enthusiasm for those with the inclination to start planting vineyards.

The book is now out of print but it was key in telling the story of wine in the UK. Skelton is the heir of those three pioneers in so many ways: establishing successful commercial vineyards in England, selecting grape varieties that do well in them, providing technical advice to those who want to make their own mark in their country's viticulture, and telling wine lovers why they should drink wines from UK vineyards and where they can go to see the revolution in action.

Chapter 2

LOCATION, LOCATION: THE RIGHT PLACE IS CRUCIAL

LOOK AT ANY GEOLOGICAL MAP THAT INCLUDES both the south of England and northern France and you will see that the same seam of chalk continues under the Channel from one country into the other. In England, it is principally in Sussex and Hampshire; in France, it is in the region around the champagne towns of Rheims and Epernay. And that, so the popular argument goes, is why sparkling wine as good as champagne can be made in England. If only life – and fizzy wine – were so simple.

With wine, so many factors influence the final result. Climate is crucial, more so than the dirt into which roots delve; vines will grow in just about any soil, but flowers won't set and grapes won't ripen if the weather

Deep in Hampshire chalk: Exton Park vineyard manager Fred Langdale and winemaker Olly Whitfield.
THE ELECTRIC EYE PHOTOGRAPHY/EXTON PARK VINEYARD

The Exton Park cellar excavation shows just how little soil lies above the Hampshire chalk. THE ELECTRIC EYE PHOTOGRAPHY/EXTON PARK VINEYARD

is too cold, too dry, too wet, too windy. Then there's the choice of vines, the variety, the specific clones, the rootstock, the density of planting – these and more affect fruit flavour as well as whether or not the plants themselves will flourish. Human involvement is another major modifying element. Other chapters in this book cover these matters, but this one is all about place.

The UK's wine vine-growing area is tiny compared to that of almost every other wine country, but within it there are major geological differences, which of course reflect in the soil that lies above the bedrock.

Sometimes that soil is nigh-on non-existent, as I found early on in the research for this book when I stood on the lip of a sheer man-cut cliff and stared down into white depths so bright that anyone working there needed to wear sunglasses. At my feet the soil was barely deep enough to nourish the roots of the short sward of downland grass. It seemed hardly possible that vines could grow in it, but they do. Below the excavation the same rock stretched down, down, down for hundreds of metres more. This was the famed Channel-hopping chalk, from the Upper Cretaceous period, laid down approximately 83 million years ago, exactly the same chalk that underlies the vineyards of the Côte des Blancs, prime chardonnay-growing area of Champagne and home to such world-renowned wines as Krug Clos du Mesnil. No wonder so many people in England latch on to the comparison.

The debate: is chalk crucial?

So many, but not everyone. In a timely, well-argued article published in *The World of Fine Wine* in November 2015, Margaret Rand, one of the most respected of wine journalists, talked to leading growers on either side. There were the chalk crusaders, led by Ian Kellett of Hambledon Vineyard (on Hampshire chalk), and the proponents of 'soil-is-the-last-thing-that-matters', with as figurehead the late Mike Roberts, founder of Ridgeview (on Sussex clay-with-limestone). Back and forth went the debate: surely it made sense to choose a soil profile as close as possible to that in Champagne if world-class sparkling wine was the aim;

Bob Lindo: 'Soil is trumped by climate every time.' CAMEL VALLEY WINES

good drainage rather than the type of soil was the all-important factor; chalk provided a finesse missing in grapes from locations elsewhere in southern England where the geology was different; exposed-to-the-wind chalk hills offered a harsher environment for vines than lower, more sheltered non-chalk sites; the capillary action of chalk combined with that of vine roots made for fitter plants as they worked hard for water they always eventually found; in a very dry summer vines would be happier rooted in clay over sand rather than in chalk; there was softer, gentler acidity in grapes grown on chalk; clay retained nutrients better; vines grown on chalk never found their roots languishing in the cold and the wet; too much chalk could be too much of a good thing for vines, yellowing their leaves due to iron deficiency.

Rand left the penultimate words to Bob Lindo, whose Camel Valley Vineyard award-winning sparkling wines are from vines rooted in ancient Cornish slate: 'England is the best experimental vineyard in the world. And soil is trumped by climate every time.' Then she countered that with the view of Nyetimber winemaker Cherie Spriggs, on the estate's Tillington single-vineyard sparkling wine (on Sussex greensand): 'It tastes of where it comes from.'

Rand's own view was summed up as she introduced the article: 'All I can say is, if you laid all the opinions in England end to end, they still wouldn't reach a conclusion. Which is probably appropriate for an industry a mere 25 years old.'

In the location debate there continues, understandably, to be much focus on southern England and its chalk downlands (though this is very modern: George Ordish's *Vineyards in England and Wales*, published in 1977 and a then highly regarded guide to wine vine-growing, included no geological discussion at all, no mention of chalk). But even the chalk isn't simple. In different places it has subtly different characteristics, affecting water retention, for example. The thickness of the soil on top of it varies from a few millimetres to many centimetres. Between the chalk hills lie other, related, base rocks. Greensand, for example, fills much of the area between the North and South Downs where the chalk has eroded and, like chalk, it is an ancient marine deposit, but its colour and characteristics are different. All this means that above and around the southern chalk there is a mosaic of soils, some sandy, some loamy, some clayey.

Move away from the south-east of England and the age of the base rocks increases, as does their variety. There are older Cretaceous layers – limestone rich in fossils, for example, which arcs from Dorset's Jurassic coast to north Yorkshire – and, edging further back in geological time, the red Devonian sandstone that covers much of the West Country. Older still are volcanic and metamorphic rocks, remnants of truly ancient volcanic activity and of the massive heat and pressure that transformed the face of the planet billions of years ago. All these create soils in which vines can flourish, so the UK is in no way short of potential growing areas, from the south to the fairly far north.

Physical evidence of all this clung to my boots as I walked the vineyards in 2017. The mud came in many colours: white, yellow, many shades of brown, deep red. There was smooth clayey mud, sandy mud, gravelly mud, mud where the pebbles or flints were too big to stick to boot soles. Sometimes it crumbled away almost immediately; on other occasions it stuck tenaciously, needing to be chipped off once it had dried. Yet vines flourished in every type of soil that created those diverse muds.

Soil – whatever the arguments for one type over another, and however much proponents may insist it affects the flavour of wine – is no more than one factor in site selection, and detailed discussion of it is best left to geologists. What else matters, perhaps even more?

High and dry or low and sheltered?

Vines hate to have their roots sitting in pools of water. For a successful crop they should grow where there is the minimum risk of frost during the delicate bud-break period. Some air movement around them is essential to reduce risks of fungal diseases, but they don't like facing into the teeth of a gale. They need a long growing season, to develop flavours in their grapes, and warm sun to ripen them. So the choice of site must largely follow the basic rules that were set many centuries ago: a well-drained slope, not too high, exposed to maximum sun but sheltered from blasting winds. That's not too difficult to achieve, certainly in southern England, and every savvy new vine-grower here should accept the criteria.

But there is argument over how much breeze vines enjoy on their leaves. At Rathfinny and Exton Park for example, both high on bare chalk hills, those responsible for the vines champion the effect of wind in reducing the risk of spring frosts or, later in the year, attacks of mildew and botrytis. Many other growers, whose vines are planted much lower, point out that their protected sites are warmer and kinder to ripening grapes. Most emphatic of the anti-wind campaigners is Peter Hall at Breaky Bottom; coincidentally, the nearest vine-growing neighbour to his sheltered South Downs site is Rathfinny.

Tweaking goes on to improve growing conditions: examples include leaving an area at the lowest point of the vineyard barren of vines to allow frost to pool there harmlessly, sparing the vines above, or creating ponds for the same effect. Windbreaks may be planted to create shelter where none occurs naturally. Digging drainage trenches in a soggy but otherwise suitable area is another possibility. But no amount of intervention, however much money is spent on it, will make a bad site good.

High on the Sussex Downs: Rathfinny Wine Estate. VIV BLAKEY/RATHFINNY WINE ESTATE

Optimum hours of sunlight, length of the growing season and overall average temperatures explain the concentration of vineyards in southern England. Not that vines can't flourish further north – George Bowden planted his Leventhorpe vineyard in Yorkshire in the 1980s, and his confidence in the potential of the south-facing slope with well-drained sandy soil has proved justified, creating immensely characterful wines, which express their complexity best after several years in bottle. Leventhorpe and its county neighbours are not the most northerly of UK vineyards – when I wrote this, one in Fife had that distinction, but it wasn't flourishing. Another, in a south-facing walled garden in Northumberland, had proved it could ripen grapes but was failing to gain much support for a crowd-funding initiative to pay for its expansion plans. So, for the moment at least, Yorkshire is the UK's not-so-frozen north so far as wine is concerned.

Vines flourish in the west, too – not only to the far tip of Cornwall and on the Isles of Scilly but also in Wales. Among the latter are plantings of white and red varieties at Ty Croes, on the southern corner of the Isle of Anglesey, its soil sandy loam over shale. They became the major focus of a 'good life' farm established by Harry Dean and his family in 1977, the vines largely pushing out the livestock, a herd of Highland cattle excepted. Glacial slopes at the foot of Snowdon are the location for Pant Du, where there is sun enough to power the entire vineyard and apple orchard operation, with spare electricity left to go to the national grid. The oldest commercial vineyard in Wales, Glyndwr, on clay above limestone soil, is in the Vale of Glamorgan, where average mean temperatures are among the highest in Britain.

But the fringes of Britain are fringe wine-lands. Even in the friendly south there can be big variations in vine-growing conditions within comparatively short distances, as research at Plumpton College, England's much-respected wine education centre, is aiming to quantify. This project, in conjunction with similar work being done at several other research institutes, should

At Breaky Bottom the sheltered north-facing vines (to the left) ripen before those on the more southerly slope. AUTHOR

have Europe-wide benefit, says Plumpton wine head Chris Foss. It is showing how even small differences between the top of a hill and the bottom, for example, can reflect substantially in vine growth.

Such detailed work is invaluable, but general principles remain. After much walking through vineyards from Kent to Cornwall, I can count on the fingers of one hand the number that faced outside the ninety-degree quadrant of south-east to south-west, but there are notable exceptions. At Breaky Bottom there is one of the rare successful north-facing English vineyards. The vines both bud earlier and produce ripe fruit sooner than their counterparts in the south-east-facing vineyard mere metres away, simply because they are more sheltered. Similarly, Denbies in the Surrey hills has a protected north-facing vineyard where pinot noir has flourished for close on thirty years; elsewhere on the estate, plantings have far more conventional exposition.

Too many would-be growers don't listen to all the advice, a situation that viticultural consultant Stephen Skelton laments: 'Sadly, there are still vineyards being planted on hopeless sites. Poor site selection is a real issue and one that is very slowly being addressed.'

As yet, there is no shortage of potential vineyard land in the UK, and it is easy to understand the attraction of this developing wine region to outsiders. For the champagne houses, expansion here makes a lot of sense, with land prices way below what they would pay at home, where availability as well as price is at a premium. The champenois interest apart, what is new in the English wine location story is that farmers who previously made other use of their land are increasingly latching on to the potential of changing to a more profitable crop. There is an increasing demand for good grapes, and canny growers on the right sites can make money from that, provided they have the resources to cover the three years between planting and the first saleable crop. As growers rather than winemakers, they don't need to invest at the eye-watering level that is required to turn grapes into quality wine, and they have the experience of coping with British weather – rain at harvest time can rot wheat as easily as grapes.

Behind the farmers, particularly those who prefer to sell their land rather than plant it, estate agents are following, and the prices they are urging sellers to ask are starting to rise steeply. Would-be vine-growers, as never before, would be wise to do their homework carefully.

Chapter 3

CLIMATE: CHANGE FOR THE BETTER, BUT PROBLEMS COME TOO

O N A GLOBAL SCALE, CLIMATE CHANGE IS TERRI-fying. On a smaller, local-to-the-UK level it is popularly considered to have made a welcome difference to wine grape-growing. But that difference is nowhere near as much for the good as it might initially appear. Higher summer temperatures are valuable, but other aspects of the change are much less favourable to UK wine producers. Our climate is increasingly given to extremes – sudden late frosts, extra-strong winds, rain in damaging deluges – and any one of these can be devastating to vines. Consider two examples. In 2012 record rainfall during flow-ering severely limited fruit set and was followed by further rain at harvest time that rotted much of the surviving yield. Many estates – of which Nyetimber was the most renowned – made no wine at all from the vintage because the quality of the remaining grapes was too poor.

In 2017 a warm and sunny early spring saw vine buds opening a fortnight or more ahead of the norm. Then in the last week of April air frost down to as low as minus 6 degrees celsius scythed through the south of England, destroying much of the new growth and leaving vineyard managers to rely on the development of secondary buds to salvage at least some grapes to harvest. Some estates lost 80 per cent of their poten-tial harvest while others were hardly affected at all. Intriguingly, 'not a bud was touched' at one of the UK's most northerly vineyards, Leventhorpe, on the outskirts of Leeds, reported owner George Bowden.

This double-edged effect is widely acknowledged. When researchers from the University of East Anglia's School of Environmental Sciences began to delve deep into the relationship between climate change and English wine in 2014, they appealed for information from all grape-growers and producers in the UK. Of the forty-two who completed the questionnaire – their 313 hectares of vineyards represented 17 per cent of the planted area of the time – 66 per cent said that climate change had, either definitely or possibly, contributed to the growth of the English wine industry. Yet, in response to a second question, asking whether they saw climate change as a threat or an opportunity, 64 per cent viewed it as a threat and a further 29 per cent considered it both a threat and an opportunity. Only the remaining 7 per cent saw climate change as an opportunity. The pessimists quoted such problems as extreme and unpredictable weather, a growing gulf between good and bad years, wind affecting physiolog-ical development, and increased disease pressure due to warm and wet growing-season weather and milder, wet winters. For the optimists, among the good points of climate change were the broader range of viable

Vine bud damaged by the April 2017 frost. ALBURY ORGANIC VINEYARD

Sunshine and stormy skies: the good and bad of climate change. ALBOURNE ESTATE

vine varieties, later harvest dates and warmer growing seasons improving yield and quality.

The 'apparent contradiction' of these replies could be explained, the researchers suggested, 'through producers' perceptions of increasing average temperature being accompanied by extreme weather events, which they attribute to change, contributing to low yield in some years'. Further understanding of that dichotomy became a key element of the continuing investigation.

Much as I'd like to summarize here all that the team, led by Alastair Nesbitt, discovered, doing so

isn't practical – there is too much else to cover. But some findings in the report, published in 2016, are very relevant to understanding the natural forces at work on present viticulture in the UK and what the future may hold. They confirmed the gradual rise in average temperatures in the growing season, April to October, from 1954 to 2013, with temperatures in southern England since 2004 frequently at least one degree above the 13 degrees celsius minimum needed for high-quality cool-climate wine grape production. (The post-2004 English temperatures are similar to those in the Champagne region through much of the second half of the twentieth century; the French growers are now facing rather more heat than they would choose, their grapes losing some of the acidity that is so crucial in making fine sparkling wine.)

Less comfortably, the research showed that temperatures in April and May have risen considerably more than the full-year average increase, encouraging the vine buds to burst open earlier and thus meaning more damage can be done by late frosts. Although these are a little rarer, they have certainly not disappeared – there was no year during the study period without at least one day in late spring when temperatures in southern England fell to a level that could harm opening buds, and these late frosts have continued since 2013. Also, the amount of rain falling in June has continued to be unpredictable, leaving unchanged the 'constant threat' that too wet a month poses to flowering, fruit set and eventual grape yield. And, warmer and wetter conditions at harvest time in October are bringing potentially more risk of disease affecting the grapes.

In essence, the general rise in growing-season temperature resulting from global warming has only a little to do with the quantity of grapes currently harvested in the UK. The continuing variability of the climate, most importantly at the crucial moment of flowering but also at bud burst and harvesting, is the major reason for the hefty fluctuations in yields from UK vineyards. In the very best years these can approach 30 hectolitres per hectare (approximately 4,000 bottles from an area the size of one and one-third football pitches), but in the worst years they struggle to reach a sixth of that. The average is around 20 hectolitres (2,700 bottles) per hectare. That same weather variability also significantly affects the quality of grapes harvested.

And one conclusion must seriously concern all those investors who in recent years have poured huge amounts of money into planting vines for sparkling wine. Alastair Nesbitt and his colleagues note the evidence suggesting that many of the grape varieties initially planted in the great UK wine revival are rather less vulnerable to poor weather than the recent favourites, chardonnay and pinot noir. Their warning is clear: 'As a result,

Rain in June remains a constant threat to flowering vines.
ALBOURNE ESTATE

the sector [sparkling wine] is now at greater risk from variability in average growing season conditions.' Perish the thought, but too many more years like 2012 might bring the downfall of some rather big names.

All vine-growers in the UK are vulnerable to weather variability, the report concludes, and they recognize that. But there is hope: 'For those investing in UK viticulture, climatic risks may be ameliorated through management strategies, market forces and their ability to cope with lower-yielding years. Projections for future climate conditions in the UK will support future risk analysis.'

What is unlikely to happen in this maritime climate is weather as extreme as that seen in some other places in the wine world. Grape vines survive cold temperatures – down to below minus 35 degrees celsius in the case of one American variety (as happens when faced with other challenges, non-vinifera vines are often sturdier than *Vitis vinifera*) – but an unusually cold snap can wreak havoc, as happened in the Finger Lakes region of New York State in January 2004. Vines that were already less than normally frost-hardy due to a combination of previous climatic factors were severely damaged or killed when temperatures fell to minus 25 degrees celsius. That cost the region's wine industry upwards of $60 million. No one is yet predicting UK winters like that, fortunately.

Similarly, the other extreme – soaring growing-season temperatures – is unlikely to occur immediately in the UK, but even a gentle increase can have adverse effects. Kevin Sutherland, winemaker at Bluebell Vineyard Estates in East Sussex, has worked in the English wine industry for close to thirty years, including a twelve-year spell teaching in the Plumpton College wine department. His prediction is that warmer, damper growing seasons will bring increasing problems for vineyard managers, with the appearance of diseases and pests never previously, or only very rarely, seen in UK vineyards. Destructive moths, for example, could fly in from Europe or hitch a lift on lorries, planes or ships, and become happily established immigrants. Vineyard managers will face greater challenges if they are to continue to produce quality fruit.

Kevin Sutherland: warmer, damper growing seasons will bring increasing problems. BLUEBELL VINEYARD ESTATES

But let's not be too dismissive of the good effects of what is happening to the weather, argues Stephen Skelton, who in his consultancy role has played such an important part in the expansion of wine grape-growing in the UK. 'Climate change has been behind much of the improvement enabling the UK to grow better quality varieties (chardonnay and pinot noir for sparkling as an example) and the quality of the "old" varieties that we still grow (bacchus, reichensteiner, seyval blanc) has also risen with the better sugar levels, lower acids and higher extract levels that you get with riper grapes.' That is due not to higher daytime temperatures alone, but also to milder nights, which mean leaves warm more quickly as day breaks and photosynthesis can begin sooner. The vine has longer to produce sugar, and the result is higher natural alcohol levels in the wine.

Temperatures will have to rise a whole lot more, however, and weather variability will need to calm down, before UK grapes ripen to the heights achieved in much hotter wine regions. Red wine at 15 degrees alcohol from rondo or regent grapes isn't likely to come from an English vineyard any time soon, and, while brandy and gin are increasingly made here from the final grape pressings, there is little possibility of a UK equivalent of port.

Look further ahead, to the end of the twenty-first century, and there could be a substantial change in both the varieties of grapes that do well in the UK and the locations of those that are already popular. Another 2016-published study, led by Professor Mark Maslin and Lucien Georgeson from University College London and commissioned by Laithwaite's Wine, combined required growing season temperatures for individual grape varieties with models of anticipated climate change to create a grape map of the UK in 2100. On it, prime pinot noir and chardonnay growing areas move north to cover a swathe of central and eastern England, from Essex to north Yorkshire. Riesling and sauvignon blanc flourish over much the same area. The heartland of pinot gris is central England and the north-east, with successful plantings there stretching from the Humber estuary to the shores of the Firth of Tay. Syrah and malbec ripen happily around the Thames estuary and parts of the Severn Valley. Merlot and tempranillo cover that area and stretch further into Kent, Sussex, Somerset and East Anglia.

Other researchers have gone even further down the global-warming route, predicting that there will be

Bush vines like these in southern France won't be seen in England for years yet. AUTHOR

Weather station recording conditions in the vineyard. ALBURY ORGANIC VINEYARD

parts of southern England – in Hampshire, Essex and Cornwall especially – where it will be too hot to grow wine grapes by 2080. Instead, they will flourish further inland, with red varieties pushing more delicate whites up to the hills or into Scotland. The most extreme suggestion is that by 2100 no vineyards at all will be left in the UK. That view wins little support in wine industry circles, but it prompted one commentator to urge action: 'We must use this narrow window of opportunity to plant our vines and drink our liquid assets while we may.'

Climate has effects beyond the choice of which vine varieties to plant. For example, it influences the style of training the vines, although the current changes are nowhere near substantial enough to alter radically what has been going on for decades. Those sturdy low-growing bush vines common in hot areas of southern Europe don't have a place in the UK, where grapes need to hang high enough off the ground to avoid the disease-promoting dampness that rises from wet soils (hence the vital importance of planting on well-drained land). Two main training systems are used for British vines: Geneva double curtain and guyot. In the former, the vine trunk is divided at a height of around 1.5 metres and two canes are trained along parallel supports, with the fruit-bearing shoots – the 'curtain' – growing downwards; it works particularly well for vigorous vines, including many of the germanic crosses long favoured in the UK. Guyot is the world's most popular vine-training system and is seen more and more frequently, as noble champagne varieties dominate the vineyards. It directs either one or two canes along a single supporting wire and from these canes the fruiting shoots grow straight up to further wires.

The space between the rows of vines is another consideration, as wider planting allows access by disease-deterring breezes. Discussion continues over the value or otherwise of leaf-plucking – removing leaves as the grapes grow, to allow more sunshine to reach them – and of green harvesting, when some of the unripe grapes are picked off to allow the remainder to ripen better. But decisions on many of these practices depend more on individual growers' preferences than on marginal changes in weather conditions.

If climate change, then, is only a small part of the reason for the burgeoning of high-quality wine in England, what else is responsible? A lot of hard work is the simplistic answer. That work includes scientific studies such as that from the University of East Anglia team, which confirms to growers the climate changes they are seeing in their vineyards and gives them a valuable tool when planning ahead, and detailed site-specific investigation, such as the Plumpton College project. And it can extend down to such basic action as preventing damage from unavoidable late frosts.

Years back, the first time I visited sparkling wine estate Ridgeview, everyone was bleary-eyed from the loss of much of the previous night's sleep. They had been out in the vineyard lighting 'bougies' – paraffin wax candles to boost air circulation around the newly budding vines and forestall the forecast frost damage. Nowadays, the preventive action can be much more sophisticated.

Bougies remain the frost-averting choice for growers who can't afford the cost of bigger, more mechanised alternatives. But there is no need now

Bougies alight at Albury Organic Vineyard in April 2017 – sadly, they didn't save the vine buds. SHEENAGH MCLAREN/ALBURY ORGANIC VINEYARD

for close attention to every spring evening's televised weather forecast. At Albury Organic Vineyard on the edge of the Surrey hills, owner Nick Wenman and his daughter Lucy Letley are examples of growers who have frost alert alarms on their mobile phones, linked to a weather station among the vines. When frost threatens, the weather station sends a text message and they can be lighting their bougies ten or fifteen minutes later. They did that in April 2017, but the candles were of little use in air temperatures of minus 4 degrees celsius, and four-fifths of the open Albury buds were destroyed.

At Gusbourne's large estate close to the Kent coast, winemaker Charlie Holland likens his eight tractor-drawn frost-busters to giant hairdryers. Set in the coldest part of the vineyard, they suck in cold air using an aeroplane-type propeller, warm it and then eject it, creating protective air circulation. Also, as relative humidity reduces, the dew point is raised significantly and frost is less likely. The machines are better than bougies, Holland says, but still not effective enough when there is serious air frost. Even more impressive is Denbies' import from New Zealand manufacturer Tow and Blow, a giant oscillating diesel-powered fan that rises up on a folding boom to nearly 10 metres above ground level and by its air-moving action can protect up to 6 hectares of vineyard. Yet again, though, this protects more against ground frost than air frost and some three-quarters of Denbies' vines were damaged in April 2017.

Intervention like this, alongside more natural solutions such as choosing a breezy site rather than a frost hollow, or creating a 'frost pool' at the lowest point of a vineyard, can go a long way towards avoiding one weather problem for UK vine-growers. But there are no preventive measures against the effects of rain at flowering or harvest. Imagine massive retractable umbrellas unfolding over English vineyards . . . at the first puff of one of those increasingly windy moments they'd be blown away.

Chapter 4

The Grapes that Make the Wine Need Careful Choice

ALMOST EVERY WINE-PRODUCING COUNTRY HAS a tradition of its own native grapes, varieties that have flourished there for millennia and are exploited with pride by modern growers. Not so the United Kingdom, at the extreme limit even now of effective vine cultivation. The varieties found here are imports, many of those grown with success brought in over the last seventy years from similarly marginal production areas. Recently, the vines of choice have changed, with plantings predominantly of the noble international varieties chardonnay and pinot noir. But until the weather warms just a little more, consistently, these will remain principally for sparkling wine production, where grapes that don't always reach their full ripeness potential are no bad thing – acidity is crucial to fizzy success. Thoughts of English still wines with the richness of Côte d'Or white burgundy or Central Otago pinot noir remain pipe-dreams, for the moment at least. Instead, the wines without bubbles continue to be made largely from grape varieties bred in Germany, which can cope with chill and dampness, provide a reasonable crop and resist the fungal diseases that the UK climate even today inevitably encourages.

These varieties are mostly crossings, often between other crossings, a technical complexity that will be of minimal interest to most wine-drinkers. But it is useful to understand a little about vines, if only to realize why some strangely named or totally unfamiliar varieties might have equally unusual flavours, or that very good wines can be made from grapes that aren't in the premier league of worldwide popularity. And it is relevant to know how the wine world separates a hybrid vine and a crossing. The former is a combination of two

Vitis riparia, one of America's wild grapes.
BILL SUMMERS @ USDA-NRCS PLANTS DATABASE

different species; the latter's components are different varieties of the same species.

The true wine grape species is *Vitis vinifera*, but there are plenty more siblings in the *Vitis* family. In North America, home of a myriad of wild vines, common varieties planted in cool areas such as New York State or Ontario belong to the *Vitis labrusca*, *Vitis aestivalis*, *Vitis rupestris* or *Vitis riparia* species, or are hybrids of these and *vinifera* – concord, norton and niagara are examples frequently grown for wine in those regions. *Vitis amurensis* is the old world's principal wild equivalent, named after the River Amur, which runs for almost 4,500 kilometres across north-east Asia.

These non-vinifera vines grow and fruit well in difficult conditions, but often the taste of wine made from their grapes suffers. The tag of 'foxy' is frequently used, although I doubt that many wine-drinkers have stuck their nose in a fox's fur to see if they agree – muskiness, earthiness, confected fruitiness are more understandable descriptions. Whatever the terminology, the drinking experience is often less than happy when set against the rounded, balanced fruitiness of well-made *Vitis vinifera* wines.

A plague on vinifera

There is, however, one particular advantage of non-vinifera vines or hybrids where the proportion of vinifera is small. In the latter part of the nineteenth century a plague hit most of Europe's major vineyard areas, its effect not unlike that of Dutch elm disease in Britain a century later. The phylloxera louse loves sucking liquid from the roots of vines, with the result that leaves wither, grapes shrivel and the plants eventually die. The offending creature is native to North America and arrived in Europe thanks to the speeding-up of transatlantic travel: before the introduction of steamships, the journey was too slow for phylloxera to survive. Once safely arrived on imported vines, the louse spread in its millions, devastating vineyards from the south of France to the north. Vins de pays or grand cru burgundies, it was indiscriminating in its voracity. From France, the plague continued into Italy, Spain and on to just about all of Europe's main wine-producing regions. An industry on which millions of people relied for their livelihood was almost completely stopped in its tracks in a handful of decades.

Myriad efforts were made to eradicate the insect. Some were bizarre, such as the application of goat's urine or garlic peel to the affected plants. Others were frightening, as in the 'scorched-earth' approach, in which highly dangerous – but ineffective – chemicals were sprayed over large areas. A few ideas, particularly the flooding of vineyards or planting in sand, seemed to work, but were totally impractical for most places where vines for fine wines flourished best.

The only true solution involved, literally, a return to the root of the problem. If cuttings from favoured *Vitis vinifera* varieties were grafted on to non-vinifera rootstocks that had a natural resistance to phylloxera, the likes of pinot noir, chardonnay, cabernet sauvignon, merlot and all the rest could – and did – flourish again throughout Europe. Ironically, those resistant rootstocks came from America's native vines, the very place from

Punch's satirization of phylloxera in 1890, in a cartoon by Edward Linley Sambourne.

which the pest itself originated. (Move forward more than a century, and phylloxera reappeared in its homeland with a vengeance, wreaking havoc in California's vineyards in the 1980s.)

While all this was happening across the Channel, vines in the UK largely escaped the plague. The first phylloxera louse recorded in the British Isles was in the unlikely location of Hammersmith, west London, in 1863. Twenty-one years later, Lord Bute's gardener spoke of 'the dreaded phylloxera so common in so many places in this country now', but, if that was true, the infestations weren't reported officially. Ministry of Agriculture records show just nine affected sites between 1863 and 1884, with two of them in Scotland, one in Eire and another in London – those three at least were unlikely places for growing wine grapes at all commercially. Each attack was rapidly halted, by grubbing up vines on the affected plots so the louse couldn't travel further. In more modern times, phylloxera appeared at Hambledon vineyard in the mid-1950s, but on grafted, and therefore resistant, vines. It could be around today, as is probably likely elsewhere in Europe, but no one mentions it as a problem.

The spread of phylloxera in the UK in pre-graft times was contained because even the areas best suited to wine grape-growing were not closely covered in vines, unlike large areas of the continent, and the vines were mostly hybrids, containing non-vinifera genes and therefore resistant. But the downside to this is that the wines, until the widespread introduction of better varieties grafted on to safe rootstocks, also inherited some of the 'foxiness' of those made from their non-vinifera ancestors. If that was the norm in wines produced in centuries past, monks and noblemen must have survived those flavours, maybe even enjoyed them, but that's certainly not the case with modern wine connoisseurs and most everyday drinkers: 'The juice will usually taste like an old potato and cabbage in your finished wine,' is how one noted English winemaker not long ago roundly dismissed a still-popular hybrid variety.

What's in the bottle and what the label can say

That's why, as wine vine-growing in the UK became more serious, and also as European wine laws came into effect, with membership of first the European Economic Community and then the European Union, hybrid vines have been outlawed in the formal 'quality' designation for still wines. (The rules for sparkling wines are somewhat different.) In recent years, many hybrids have been replaced by more favoured vinifera varieties and few are now planted.

Change hasn't happened overnight. There has been a lengthy period of transition, largely since the introduction from the 1991 vintage of the Quality Wine scheme. It took time for existing growers to adapt to new requirements with minimal effect on their income (though a sensible income from English wine is very far from guaranteed: the UK must surely be home of the adage that to make a small fortune from wine you need a very large one to start with). From 2011 the rules were tightened, with specific requirements for sparkling as well as still wines. The hierarchy, from the top downwards, is English and Welsh Quality Wine with 'protected designation of origin' (PDO), English and Welsh Regional Wine with 'protected geographical indication' (PGI), Varietal Wine (still) that is allowed to name the place of origin but not to state 'English' or

English PDO Quality Sparkling Wine, from Camel Valley.
CAMEL VALLEY WINES

'Welsh' on the labels, and the rest, UK Wine, where labelling rules are as for Varietal Wine but without mention of vintage or variety. The top two levels must be tested and tasted before being labelled, and makers of Varietal Wine must provide the information required for their wines to be so certified.

Essentially, non-vinifera grapes are banned from non-sparkling PDO English or Welsh Quality Wines, though there are newer hybrids (known as 'interspecific crosses') that are considered to be vinifera grapes and thus are allowed. English and Welsh PDO Quality Sparkling Wines may be made only from six named varieties, chardonnay, pinot noir, pinot meunier, pinot gris, pinot blanc and pinot noir précoce. But Quality Sparkling Wines (without the PDO) can be made from any grape variety grown in the UK, as can wines in the non-'quality' categories. And all these wines must be made from fresh, UK-grown grapes. Phew! Wine legislation is complex.

The main varieties, from bacchus to rondo

The choice of varieties that now go into these categories of wines, while very different from the 1990s, is still something of a mix. So it makes sense to look at the main grapes that grow here, what they are used for and how they taste.

Despite plentiful historical references to red wines – there is one, for example, that asserts that a red from Sussex in the eighteenth century was 'very good and resembled burgundy' – the UK in the twenty-first century is very much white wine country. The fact that a red grape, pinot noir, is right at the top of the planting table alongside chardonnay doesn't herald a burgundian-style red revolution. It is there thanks to the success of English sparkling wine, and, as with chardonnay, little pinot noir ends up as still wine. Of the dozen grapes that follow this pair in the popularity league, only four (none more than 5 per cent of the total plantings) are red. One of those four, pinot meunier, is used only in sparkling wine, which is also the main destination of early-ripening pinot noir précoce. With the 'champagne' grapes now occupying more than half of the vineyard area and winemakers filling at

least two out of every three bottles with sparkling wine, no wonder that a mere 10 per cent of English wine is red or rosé.

Among the whites intended for still wines, bacchus is often considered Britain's answer to New Zealand sauvignon blanc. It seems set to retain third place in the planting table, and is a favoured choice by growers whose target is still rather than sparkling wines. Could it become as important to UK growers as sauvignon blanc is to the Kiwis? That's unlikely, given the dominance of sparkling wine, but it is increasingly the favoured variety for still white wines.

Bacchus is one of the multi-generation *Vitis vinifera* crossings and has a promising pedigree: one parent is a cross of sylvaner and riesling, the other is the riesling-derived müller-thurgau. It is a much more recent German creation than its parents, dating from 1972. It comes firmly into the category of good inventions. Well-made bacchus wines are aromatic, fruity and crisp and have potential to age; flavours vary according to picking time and are often likened to those of Kiwi or Loire Valley sauvignon blanc. Also, there can be fine sweet wines made from it, when botrytis (noble rot) develops on grapes left late on the vine. For the grower, bacchus is less effusively vigorous than many crosses/hybrids and isn't as disease-prone as some, but as with every wine grape there are problems with fruit set if the weather is cold or wet at flowering time.

In the right hands, the variety's prospects are promising indeed. In 2015, Albourne Estate's 2014 bacchus

Bacchus grapes ripening at Redbank Vineyard. RICHARD GRIFFITHS/SIXTEEN RIDGES

was named English Wine of the Year, beating more than 320 other wines, sparklers included. Remarkably, that wine was only the second vintage from Albourne, where Alison Nightingale had planted, from 2010, a range of grape varieties on 10 hectares of a greensand ridge overlooking the South Downs close to Brighton. In 2016, another bacchus, from Winbirri Vineyards in Norfolk, took the same title. Again, there was proof that English wine isn't all about bubbles, and again the wine was from young vines.

A much, much bigger accolade came in May 2017, when that same Winbirri 2015 bacchus was declared the best-value white wine made from any single grape variety in the Decanter World Wine Awards and carried off one of the thirty-four Platinum Best in Show awards. With more than 17,200 wines from around the world

Lee Dyer receives the 2016 English Wine of the Year award for Winbirri Bacchus from Jonathan Bourne-May, Worshipful Company of Vintners. WINEGB

Alison Nightingale with 2015 English Wine of the Year, Albourne Estate Bacchus. ALBOURNE ESTATE

entered, that was a remarkable success for a 5-hectare English vineyard growing a variety that much of the wine world had never heard of – it put East Anglia 'on the world stage of winemaking', a competition spokeswoman commented. Its maker, Lee Dyer, believes that his region is ideal bacchus-land, with good ripening encouraged by sunnier and much drier autumns than those enjoyed in counties bordering the English Channel.

While bacchus is increasing in the UK and is comfortably the third most popular grape, the noble champagne varieties are pushing out most other white varieties. Among those, seyval blanc is the one that prompts most disagreement among growers and drinkers – it's the grape that was condemned for those raw potato and cabbage flavours by Owen Elias. His forthright grape glossary on his English Terroir blog adds that it is 'most hideous and boring', and he used the word 'hideous' again when I dared ask in 2017

Owen Elias at Nutbourne Vineyards, with owner Bridget Gladwin.
AUTHOR

whether his view had changed. Elias's opinion should be taken seriously – he was head winemaker for ten years at the biggest UK wine producer, Chapel Down, has worked at a host of other important vineyards, has been named UK Vineyards Association winemaker of the year four times, and has made more than three million bottles of English wine. He does concede, however, that there are very rare examples of good seyval blanc.

But others like seyval blanc's generous cropping, its reliability even in poor years, its resistance to disease, and also its flavour, considering it mildly citrussy rather than vegetal. They believe it is a good all-rounder, with an acidity that contributes much in the making of sparkling wines particularly. The seyval wines, initially still but since 1996 all sparkling, from Peter Hall at Breaky Bottom in East Sussex are highly regarded and much medalled. 'Elegant, sweet-natured' is his description of the variety. Compared to fruitier germanic varieties, seyval 'gives a cleaner more open taste, a balance between vinosity with a touch of fruit', Hall says. He was delighted to discover the grape soon after he began planting at Breaky Bottom in the 1970s, as he aimed to replicate fine wines from the Loire Valley but found the French varieties unhappy even in his sheltered niche of the South Downs. Another multi-medal-winning example of sevyal is as an important component of Camel Valley Cornwall Brut, the flagship wine of Cornwall's largest vineyard. Its makers, the Lindo

family, laud it for its 'English hedgerow scents and a touch of honey on the palate'.

Seyval blanc is not one of the hybrid grape varieties now accepted as *Vitis vinifera*. It predates them, originating in France in the 1920s, a combination of American-based grape varieties that had been developed by the prolific vine breeder Albert Seibel in the aftermath of phylloxera. It takes its name from its creator, Bertille Seyve, and the Villiard vine-breeding family into which he married. Raymond Barrington Brock and Edward Hyams both grew it successfully and it was the most-planted UK variety not that many years ago. How wine fashions change.

Reichensteiner, planted today in similarly small quantities – on just below 5 per cent of vineyard land – is, like bacchus, a result of vinifera crossings. One parent is müller-thurgau, the other was born of table grapes madeleine angevine (confusingly, there is also a wine grape of the same name, related but different) and early calabrese (which is, despite its name, a grape, not a brassica). Early vigour reduces with age, it stays reasonably free of disease, yields well and is useful in blends and as a base for sparkling wines, prompting a small revival in recent years. David and Linda Carr Taylor, who farm 15 hectares inland from Hastings in East Sussex, planted reichensteiner in 1971 and have remained enthusiastic, saying it is 'probably our most successful variety in terms of reliable cropping and ripening and grows very well on our site'. The Carr Taylors confirm its value in sparkling wine – they were the first modern UK growers to make commercial quantities of wine following the classic champagne-style practice of second fermentation in bottle, a move prompted by an exceptionally generous harvest of reichensteiner in 1983.

How the mighty have fallen applies even more to müller-thurgau than to seyval blanc. In the 1950s and 1960s, those two varieties shouldered out just about all challengers, but now müller-thurgau vines comprise barely 3 per cent of the UK total. Müller-thurgau, developed in Germany in the late nineteenth century, has a complicated background, but seems most likely to be a combination of two variants of riesling. German

Ortega ready to harvest at Denbies.
DENBIES WINE ESTATE

growers used to love it – it's the Liebfraumilch grape – and it was New Zealand's widest-planted variety for a while, before being drowned in a sea of sauvignon blanc. Raymond Barrington Brock believed it was one of his most successful introductions: it was 'known to give an outstandingly fine wine in cool climates'.

Now, that view has changed: 'It properly belongs to a different era,' argues Owen Elias. Disadvantages include difficult-to-control vigour, low yields and very little disease resistance. When there were clean, healthy, ripe grapes – a rare occurrence – good-quality wines could be made across a range of styles, he continues. But most often it proved 'flabby and dull'. In *Wine Growing in Great Britain* (2014), Stephen Skelton agreed: 'With hindsight, it was a variety that the UK could probably have done without.' The best examples could be excellent, with good fruity flavours, he comments; in poor, underripe years the tendency was 'towards the herbaceous and catty'.

Of other germanic white grapes, ortega has plenty of fans, often for its potential in sweet wines. Ortega is another vinifera cross, of müller-thurgau with siegerrebe, a very early ripening and aromatic grape occasionally seen in the UK. (Siegerrebe has keen followers – Three Choirs Vineyard in particular – who enjoy its muscat aromatics and versatility, but if allowed to ripen too much, its attraction for wasps and birds is a decided disadvantage.) Like its parent, ortega is ready to pick sooner than many varieties, so its early flowering

means spring frosts can be a big problem. However, if it escapes disease and ripens well, noble rot will often set in, lending a characteristic marmalade-y sweetness to the resulting wine. Dry ortega can be successful as well, and the wine has enough richness to age happily in oak, something that doesn't work with many of the lighter, more acidic white grapes.

Denbies, for decades England's largest single-vineyard wine producer, has made a successful late-harvest dessert wine from ortega in several recent vintages, with the 2011 winning a gold medal in the International Wine Challenge and a regional trophy in the Decanter World Wine Awards. From the excellent 2016 harvest it chose also to make a limited-edition cuvée to celebrate the estate's thirtieth anniversary – a gloriously intense mouthful of sweet liquid gold that I was privileged to taste from the single barrel. At Biddenden Vineyards in the Kent Weald, ortega is the signature variety, with more than half of the 9-hectare vineyard devoted to it. The off-dry wines have received many medals, the highest a Decanter World Wine Awards silver for the 2014 vintage, admired by the judges for its 'marvellously flavoursome style with a delightful honeyed character . . . [evoking] Alsace in May!'.

More experimental are the plantings of solaris, a white grape that is yet another German crossing. Its parentage is far too complicated to detail here, but one grandparent was red, an Asiatic wild grape. Despite those wild genes, solaris is defined as an interspecific

Assistant winemaker Andy Kershaw draws Denbies' late-harvest ortega dessert wine from the barrel. AUTHOR

cross and thus accepted as *Vitis vinifera*. Denbies has 'great hopes for this variety', said chief executive officer Chris White, following a promising maiden harvest in 2016, from vines planted in 2013. Solaris has been the main choice at two newer vineyards away from the southern heartland of English wine: Frithsden, between Hemel Hempstead and Tring in Hertfordshire, and Llaethliw, at the foot of the Cambrian mountains on the west coast of Wales. All three producers like it for its early ripening (late September) and good resistance to fungal diseases and frost, plus, in the words of Denbies, the 'intensely flavoured, rounded and mellow' wine that results. Solaris is another variety with dessert wine potential.

There are more grapes developed from parents native to various parts of Europe and beyond to be seen in UK vineyards – huxelrebe, madeleine angevine (the wine grape, not the table grape), phoenix, scheurebe and schönburger are the main examples – and vine scientists, particularly in Switzerland and Germany, are working on further crossings. They are smilingly known as piwis, from a shortening of the complicated German word for 'disease resistance'. These are the new grapes that now mostly are regarded as vinifera rather than hybrids. But many UK growers believe that better non-sparkling white wines could, as time goes on, come from nobler white grapes.

Pinot blanc is one, 'an ideal grape for England', says Owen Elias, who has been responsible for planting it at a number of vineyards, including Chapel Down. The best results can be very stylish, but there are not yet many examples around. Pink-tinged pinot gris, with its spicier edge, is more fashionable than its white cousin beyond UK shores, and it is becoming more popular here. Both blanc and gris flourish in the sandy soil of Stopham Vineyard, close to Pulborough on the edge of the South Downs. Stopham is another of the English vineyards to enjoy royal favour – its fine pinot blanc was one of three English wines served on the Royal Barge during Queen Elizabeth II's Diamond Jubilee celebrations in 2012 and surely must have been much appreciated, even on that chilly, soggy day.

Sauvignon blanc and riesling have a few supporters, and chenin blanc could join them, but as yet England's weather isn't right: success with such varieties, says Stephen Skelton, remains 'a pipe-dream in all but the

Pinot blanc.
STOPHAM VINEYARD

very ripest of vintages'. Wait a little, counters Chris Foss, head of the wine department at Plumpton College, and that will certainly change. Denbies has already released a sauvignon blanc/bacchus blend and is happy with the variety, as is another Surrey vineyard, Greyfriars, which includes a sauvignon blanc sparkling wine in its core range. But Rathfinny has pulled up the riesling it planted on its open Sussex downland estate, after it failed to reach full phenolic ripeness. 'We just couldn't get the flavour,' admitted Mark Driver, who is owner, with his wife Sarah, of what is set to become most probably England's largest single vineyard, once its 180 hectares are fully planted. There are promising small-scale experiments in Kent with albariño, best known from Spain's green north, and it too has been blended with bacchus to good effect. Then, of course, there are all those hectares of chardonnay. Very nearly all the grapes go into sparkling wine, but, in the right place with the right weather, good still wines can be made. Chapel Down and Gusbourne in Kent, Nutbourne in West Sussex and Lyme Bay in Devon are among producers proving that.

Moving on to red grapes, there is that same potential for pinot noir, which, like chardonnay, is at present mostly intended for fizz. Raymond Barrington Brock's trials with it were disappointing, but that seemed not to deter early experimenters, even though they struggled to produce any decent wine. Even now it is recognized as a difficult grape to grow – Gusbourne winemaker Charlie Holland has described it as 'hard to master . . . infamously fussy' – but a few growers have regularly been getting still pinot noir right. Bolney Estate is one of them, with a delicate, perfumed wine that has true pinot character. Sixteen Ridges also achieves that character with pinot noir précoce and Gusbourne's still pinot noir is a very fine wine, as stylish as the fizz into which more of the estate's grapes go. I have also tasted a barrel sample with great potential from Lyme Bay, made with grapes grown in Essex.

Intriguingly for a grape still at the edge of its comfortable growing zone, there has been a recent move to up-market styles. Eyebrows were raised early in 2017 when Litmus Wines – which combines

Pinot noir. GUSBOURNE

wine consultancy with wine production, at Denbies – released its 2014 pinot noir at a recommended retail price of £30–£35. Its maker, John Worontschak, followed a very classic burgundian path with the wine, both fermenting and ageing it in oak barrels. It sold out immediately, with a quarter bought by Marks & Spencer before its official release. Another smart English pinot noir in that price range, Black Ewe from Trevibban Mill, inland from Padstow in Cornwall, took a silver medal in the International Wine Challenge with its 2014 vintage.

Will other classic red grapes make their mark in England? On 1 April 2017, London online wine merchant Honest Grapes issued a press release revealing that top Saint-Emilion grower Jonathan Maltus was about to plant merlot vines in his home county of Kent. Yes, it was an April Fools' joke, but perhaps not so very far from the possible truth. It will be intriguing to see if in due course the winemakers of Bordeaux follow their colleagues from Champagne and start to buy land and plant red grapes in southern England. A little cabernet sauvignon and merlot is already grown in England, but under poly tunnels.

For the moment, most English red is made from far less familiar varieties – their origins, again, generally lying in Germany. The most frequently planted, rondo, is something of an exception, however, with vines in its family tree coming from Manchuria and Austria. The dark red wine that results from the final cross – classified as vinifera despite those very mixed origins – tastes properly vinous; Skelton likens it to a cross between tempranillo and syrah.

Rondo does pretty well in the UK, if its vigorous growth is cut back enough to allow sun to reach the grapes. It has good frost resistance, ripens early and adds welcome colour to the English red palette. However, both Skelton and Elias reckon that finer wines can be made from regent, another grape with hybrid genes alongside dominating vinifera ones from white germanic varieties, and an example from the piwi stable. The hybrid parent is vigorous, productive, wet-weather-tolerant chambourcin, again a Seyve family invention and a vine seen in such disparate locations as France's Loire Valley, Australia and Vietnam. Regent wine has good colour, medium acidity, manageable tannins and dark fruit aromas; the vine is disease-resistant and its fruit ripens well. More is being planted, and its popularity is growing in Germany, too.

In Germany there is even greater enthusiasm for dornfelder, which, *The Oxford Companion to Wine* notes, 'incorporates every important red wine vine grown in Germany somewhere in its genealogy and happily seems to have inherited many more of their good points than their bad'. Provided they can keep its yields under control, some UK growers are discovering those good points – notably its decent colour, good acidity and smooth texture – especially when blended with other reds. At its best, suggests Skelton, expect a spicy Rhône style, but he doesn't see a great UK future for the variety. Ageing in barrels works well with all of this trio of reds.

There is one other important classic red grape in England. Pinot meunier has a very long way to go before it reaches anywhere near the abundance of its two companions-in-champagne, chardonnay and pinot noir. It is 'woefully under-represented', bemoans Elias, who stresses its reliability compared to England's top two vines, its tolerance of a wider range of sites and a greater resistance to frost damage. His view is contested by some others, who see it as the trickiest of the trio to grow. Surely, though, as the inexorable rise of fizz continues, there will be more, and existing enthusiasts have been smiling lately.

'The pinot meunier was the highlight; terrific flavours, great sugar levels but still good acidity,' wrote Rathfinny's Mark Driver as the 2016 grapes reached the winery. This was the estate's first major harvest – 79.5 tonnes – from vines planted in 2012. Exton Park's head winemaker Corinne Seely made the UK's first-ever pinot-meunier-only rosé traditional-method sparkling wine and saw it garlanded with medals in the months after its launch in 2016. She believes the grape has potential on Hampshire chalk, even though it needs careful handling. A 'naughty teenager' is her view of it, and she has adopted a chablis-inspired pruning system to tame its errant ways. At Bride Valley in Dorset, Bella Spurrier remarks on the extra character pinot meunier gives, and both the classic blend Brut Reserve and the Rosé Bella include it in quite generous proportions.

Of course, different varieties of grapes have different

Dornfelder grapes at the start of veraison – the stage when grape berries swell, soften and their skin changes colour.
STOPHAM VINEYARD

flavours, changed somewhat by the degree of ripeness at which they are picked. Flavours can be modified, too, by other factors: the soil in which the vines are grown, the exposition or slope of the vineyard, the local climate. Those create what is known as the 'terroir' effect, and terroir is one of the biggest areas of discussion – and often disagreement – between wine professionals. Only minerality – the fact (or fiction) that geology can be tasted in wine – inspires more heated debate. Terroir certainly has its place in this celebration of English wine: turn back to Chapter 2.

Enemies of the grapes

To return to the vines themselves, in this account of those varieties that grow in the UK there has been frequent mention of susceptibility to disease and of how well or otherwise grapes ripen. Both factors are crucial in the challenge for everyone who is part of, or wants to join, the growing band of serious, successful wine producers.

These issues have always confronted growers. The Romans went to great lengths to ensure the grapes they grew were of good quality, as the pollen from weeds of cultivation at Wollaston vineyard excavation hints. There, archaeologist Ian Meadows suggests, the earth between the rows of vines was quite likely deliberately hoed free of other vegetation, as bare soil is better at absorbing the sun's warmth and reflecting it back, contributing to ripening. From the Romans onwards, English wine vine-growers have often struggled for ripeness, as the many records of poor harvests prove. Time and again, growers have been told to plant on sheltered slopes exposed to the sun and with free-draining soils; all too frequently, even recently, such sensible recommendation has been ignored.

Disease is rather a different matter. While as early as the seventeenth century wide spacing between both individual vines and rows of vines was recommended, to prevent damage induced by mist or heavy dew, it was not until the nineteenth century that two truly harmful diseases, both forms of mildew, arrived. Again, the source of the problem was America and, again,

'Naughty teenager' pinot meunier vines ready for pruning at Exton Park Vineyard. AUTHOR

native American vines showed good resistance while *Vitis vinifera* was badly hit. Both powdery mildew (also known as oidium) and downy mildew attack the leaves and other soft green parts of the vine, leading to poor fruit set and, with the former, spoiled grapes that can ruin the flavour of wines made from them.

Powdery mildew made its first recorded appearance in Europe at Margate in Kent, where in 1845 John Tucker, gardener on a local estate, noticed diseased leaves on some of the vines he tended. Downy mildew arrived a little later, after first being reported in south-west France in 1878. It spread across Europe as rapidly as phylloxera and was almost as significant in its effect. But, unlike phylloxera, both mildews were soon to be defeated by plant scientists. For powdery mildew, dusting with sulphur was the solution, a largely preventive treatment needing several applications during the growing

Vine mildew, from a nineteenth-century French treatise by Gustave Fron on plant diseases.

season. For the downy, a mixture of copper sulphate and lime – the famed turquoise-coloured Bordeaux mixture whose traces can still be seen on the exteriors of many old, vine-clad French houses – did the job, both killing off the fungus and preventing its reappearance.

Vines also suffer another somewhat similar infection – grey mould or *Botrytis cinerea* – but this is loved as well as hated by winemakers. Arriving early it overwhelms the vine with its furry coat; delaying until grapes are ripe it creates the 'noble rot' that shrivels the berries, concentrates their sweet juice and adds a unique flavour to the finished wine. England has a way to go to reach the heights of Sauternes or the wonderful chenin blanc stickies of the Loire Valley, but more good noble rot sweet wines are appearing. Unlike the comparatively non-toxic character of the sprays against the two mildews, however, those developed

for unwanted botrytis have been the cause of concern over possible risk of residues appearing in wine from treated grapes. Stephen Skelton argues, however, that the 'revolution' of those botrytis-fighters has been a real benefit to growers, giving them much better control over a disease that can wipe out a huge percentage of their crop in a matter of days: 'No one mentions this in relation to higher alcohol levels – but higher alcohol levels have much to do with longer hang-time due to better disease control.'

Alternatives to the chemical route

Chemicals are a contentious issue. Influential voices in the English wine revival have lauded the arrival of more sophisticated, effective sprays as the route to effective commercial wine grape-growing in a marginal climate. Many of the new wave of committed makers of high-quality sparkling wine are convinced that it is impossible to produce wine grapes satisfactorily year-on-year, even in the warmer parts of the UK, without resource to spraying against disease.

Does that have to be the way to go? One who has argued firmly that it does not is Monty Waldin, a respected voice in print and on television, a judge for several years at the United Kingdom Vineyards Association Wine of the Year awards and the first writer to specialize in organic and biodynamic wine. In *Biodynamic Wines*, published in 2004, he was scathing about the spray-first, think-later attitude: 'Sadly, Britain's 400-odd wine-growers appear more interested in lobbying the European Union to sanction the use of a much wider range of synthetic anti-rot and anti-mildew sprays than they are in organics.' But things could be different, he suggested: 'The trick is to educate British consumers to realize that British vineyard soils have never been used as a dumping ground for town refuse, unlike those of Champagne, and that UK wine-growers can be environmental stewards, not environmental thieves.'

Such ambition is far from new, and it relates not just to how the vines themselves are treated. Doing unpleasant things to wine has been going on for many

Healthy grapes grown without resource to herbicides and pesticides. ALBURY ORGANIC VINEYARD

the chemical route completely, and those who still follow it tend to take greater care in the amount of spray they use and how often they apply it. Many, for example, have bought sophisticated spraying machines that collect and reuse the surplus rather than allowing it to fly away on the wind, and many have abandoned the use of herbicides, leaving their vineyards looking altogether greener. Read on, and there will be more about different approaches to vine-growing.

Furred and feathered threats

Organic or conventional, vineyards in the UK face animal as well as vegetal attack on their ripening grapes. Few ordinary gardeners would count blackbirds, thrushes or starlings as pests, but to the grape-grower they certainly are. A flock can quickly pillage the best grapes, moments before picking. Netting is one solution, but it is expensive, time-consuming to put in place and risks fatally trapping small birds. Even ground-feeding birds such as pheasants and partridges can be a problem. Many growers train and prune their vines so the fruiting branches are too high off the ground for these two predators to reach, although pheasants are adept at stretching and fluttering up to tempting bunches. Noisy bird scarers are another approach. Often, growers choose to shrug off such attacks, and those by wasps, as a part of the inevitable hazards en route to the winery.

Rabbits and deer do need to be taken seriously, however, for they can cause severe damage to the vines themselves. Country-wide, rabbit guards protect just about every newly planted vine. In Hampshire and Sussex, deer fences surround most vineyards to keep out the most destructive of animal invaders. Kent is largely free of deer, but wild boar have returned to the county and roam clumsily through planted areas, breaking vine branches and sometimes tasting the fruit. Fortunately, English grapes are rarely ripe enough to properly satisfy the boars' desire for ultimate sweetness. Badgers, too, have a sweet tooth and can cause damage as well as fruit loss when they rest their paws on support wires and munch away. Who would be a vine-grower. . . ?

centuries. George Ordish, in the historic survey which begins his *Vineyards in England and Wales* (1977), refers to the 'first complete printed book entirely devoted to wine', published in Italy in 1480. Its author, thought to be a professor in Bologna, 'recommended such substances as white clays, egg-whites, vine roots, juniper roots and berries, wheat, hops, ivy leaves, pine needles, sand, willow bark, hyssop, comfrey, dittany, parsley, leek seed, nettles, powdered deer horn, and powdered rue seed' as additions to wine. But those, counters Ordish, 'may have been better than some of today's measures with the cheaper wines, such as stuffing them full of sulphur dioxide gas in order to ensure that they remain bright, unalterable, sterile (and dead) for years'. All winemakers who work organically (and there are now rules for organic wineries as well as for organic vineyards) would echo that anti-sulphur sentiment.

When Monty Waldin lamented the pro-chemical attitude of so many of the UK's wine grape-growers, he knew of only two whose vineyards were certified as organic. But between then and now there has been some change in attitude. More growers are eschewing

Chapter 5

From Grape to Bottle, the Process of Making Wine

S O THE GRAPES ARE RIPE AND READY TO BE PICKED. What happens next? The generally accepted theory is that speed is of the essence: grapes off the vine, into small boxes (to minimize premature crushing) and away to the winery for pressing before oxygen has had a chance to work its flavour-affecting worst. That's fine when the winery is alongside the vineyard. As at Exton Park in Hampshire, where head winemaker Corinne Seely says: 'It's five minutes from vineyard to press. It would be crazy to lose that freshness.' Or at Stopham in West Sussex, where Simon Woodhead's grapes grow just across a farm track from his press and tanks. Both are determined to avoid oxidation of the juice from their carefully tended grapes.

But, with 500-plus vineyards in the UK and little more than a quarter of that number of wineries, such proximity isn't the norm. For example, Lyme Bay Winery in east Devon uses fruit from Kent and Essex, Gusbourne brings grapes from its second vineyard in West Sussex to the Kent winery, and even Nyetimber transports all its grapes, from both the West Sussex estate and its Hampshire vineyards, to its winery at Crawley.

Yet there aren't loads of oxidized wines around. Gusbourne winemaker Charlie Holland explains why English grapes survive even quite lengthy journeys: 'They're pretty hard.' Lyme Bay's Liam Idzikowski echoes that: 'They don't squish.' Idzikowski adds a further, forthright fact, so different from the situation in warm-climate wine countries: 'We're picking in October, and it's bloody cold.' Even so, Lyme Bay's furthest-flung fruit is in the winery and pressed within twelve hours of leaving the vine. Overall, emphasizes Holland, 'the best thing is to keep the grapes intact

Freshly picked chardonnay grapes from the Windsor Great Park Vineyard ready to head for the winery. STEVEN MORRIS/LAITHWAITE'S WINE

and then get them into the tank as soon as possible after pressing'.

Once the grapes have arrived safely in the winery, whether from a few hundred metres or many scores of kilometres away, the process of turning them into wine begins. The basic theory is very simple. Alcohol results from the action of yeast on sugar. Grapes contain sugar. Squeeze out the juice, put it into a container, leave it and, because of naturally occurring yeast on skins and stalks, even in the air around, fermentation happens and wine is produced.

Of course, in any winery the process is much more closely controlled, for reliable results. This isn't the place to go into the detail of that, so here is just a brief overview, concentrating on still white and sparkling wines as they are so much the emphasis in the UK. Making red wine follows generally similar principles, although skins stay with the juice during fermentation and are left to macerate in it afterwards so that the wines achieve the necessary colour and depth of flavour.

From grape to juice: a gentle squeeze

Pressing the grapes, after such unwanted bits and pieces as twigs, dead insects and rotting berries have been removed, is the first stage. Various types of press are in use in the UK, with the new wave of sparkling winemakers generally choosing those favoured for champagne. Coquard is the classic French choice, a sophisticated, gentle version of the traditional basket press; alternatives are soft-action pneumatic presses. For those winemakers most fanatical about avoiding oxidation, a press that blankets the grapes with inert nitrogen is the must-buy style. Bucher is the best known and there will surely be more of its presses in England, but the pace has been set by Exton Park, Simpsons and Coates & Seely. Winemakers at these three estates love the precise control that these presses offer. 'You can see the difference in colour according to whether you are using nitrogen or not,' notes Exton Park head wine-maker Corinne Seely, who insisted on equipment that allows her to press her grapes very, very slowly indeed. Wine from grapes pressed under inert gas has a very citrussy, granny-smith-apple character, says Charles Simpson, while using a more oxidative process for the same grapes will give a more tropical character, with mango and pineapple flavours.

Whatever type of press is used, normally several fractions of juice result. The first runs out freely simply

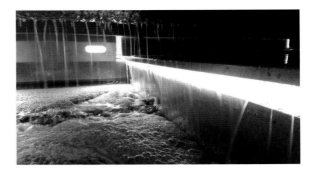
Juice bubbles from the press at Redbank winery.
SIMON DAY/SIXTEEN RIDGES

because of the weight of the grapes in the press; the next follows gentle pressure; and the final portion is the result of harder pressing. For growers making both sparkling and still wines, having different fractions of juice is no problem. The earlier parts go to make the base wine for fizz; the later pressings, which have greater flavour, are good for still wine. Makers of still wine can also use all fractions. If there is no room for still wine on a producer's list, there are other possibilities for the later pressings – English gin and eau de vie are increasingly popular winery by-products.

The pressed juice then goes into stainless steel tanks, or occasionally oak barrels, is chilled to allow impurities to settle out, and – very frequently for English wine – sugar is added (the technical term for this is chaptalization). The sweeter the juice, the more alcoholic the finished wine will be. Decades back, English wine was very low in alcohol, often below 10 per cent, which meant that frequently it was unpalatably acidic. Warmer growing seasons and riper grapes are putting paid to that issue, but a little sweetening to raise the final alcohol level (the permitted maximum resulting increase is 3 per cent, less for organic and biodynamic wines) helps achieve today's 11–12 per cent wines, with more rounded yet still refreshingly crisp flavours.

Beware of letting nature take its course

The fermentation that happens without any human intervention if newly pressed grape juice is left sitting

Grapes go into the press at Albourne Estate. ALBOURNE ESTATE

in a tank is a risky process. It can take a very long time, there may be interruptions when all activity stops, and the final flavours may not be what the winemaker wants. Hence the importance of cultivated yeasts in the wine industry worldwide. Winemakers need the right one for their particular product, from an enormous choice. There are plenty of yeasts developed for cool-climate areas such as the UK, although anyone making organic wines has to use those from organic sources and for biodynamic certification only natural 'wild' yeasts are allowed. With the chosen yeast added, the wine-to-be bubbles away until the sugar is gone and fermentation stops.

That is pretty close to the end of the process for still wines, although if extra flavour is wanted the wine is left for a while on its lees, the dead yeast cells and other solids resulting from fermentation. It is moved to a clean tank, leaving behind that layer of yeasty sediment, in a process known as 'racking', then fined and filtered to clear out any tiny particles that would lead to it looking cloudy or perhaps cause contamination. Finally, it is bottled. The agents used in fining determine whether the finished wines are suitable for vegetarians and vegans; for example, they can include gelatin, milk protein or isinglass from fish bladders, or non-animal-based materials such fine clay or pea protein. The less intrusive the approach at this time, the more the wine retains its character. Along the way from picked grape to bottle, the wine is protected from risk of contamination by the addition of a little sulphur

dioxide, with the allowed limits set lower for organic and biodynamic wines.

There can be one extra step either during alcoholic fermentation or immediately afterwards: malolactic conversion. This can occur without human intervention but more usually is prompted by the deliberate addition of lactic acid bacteria that change the naturally occurring, very sharp malic acid in the wine into softer lactic acid. Whether winemakers choose to go down this route depends on the final style they are seeking and the practice is much more common in reds than whites. Overdo it, and the wine can have almost a sour cream character or the heavy butteriness that was once a characteristic of much Australian chardonnay. Most extensive debate on the use of malolactic conversion in the UK comes among makers of sparkling wine. Some say it is to be avoided like the plague, so the final fizz is quintessentially crisply English; others find the result is just too acidic if malolactic conversion isn't done.

Putting the bubbles in the bottle

Such mention of fizz leads neatly to how England's sparkling wines are created. More and more English fizz comes from the three champagne varieties, chardonnay, pinot noir and pinot meunier. Two of these are red, so how come most of the wine is white? The secret lies in taking away the skins of the red grapes from the juice (which is white, not red – very few red grapes actually have red juice) as quickly as possible. Sometimes, though, a little skin contact is wanted, for a rosé result. Alternatively, a pink colour can be achieved, perfectly legally, by adding a dash of red wine to the white fizz.

The classic three-C grapes aren't the only choice. Excellent sparkling wines are also made from seyval blanc, as those from Breaky Bottom and Camel Valley have proved, and some newer producers also like the grape. Seyval is suitable because it isn't strongly aromatic. Occasionally other germanic varieties are used, most often in blends. There are sparkling whites in which sauvignon blanc or bacchus is the sole or largest component, and the occasional red fizz is made

Work at all levels in the Gusbourne winery. GUSBOURNE

English sparkling wine: second fermentation in bottle is the route to quality. CAMEL VALLEY WINES

from dornfelder or rondo. But the champagne varieties will continue to dominate massively, consultant Stephen Skelton insists: 'Why look elsewhere for making sparkling? Champagne hasn't for hundreds of years. Chardonnay and pinot noir have a level of public understanding and acceptance that outweighs any other consideration.'

Whatever the grapes used, the process – the traditional second-fermentation-in-bottle method most famous from champagne – is the same. Linda Carr Taylor, whose family was responsible for making the first commercial English sparkling wine, explains why: 'It's really the only way to produce sparkling wine of quality.'

The base wine for a sparkling result is made very much as a normal still wine is, though usually the most heavily pressed juice fraction is not included. Most sparkling wine producers keep the grapes from each of their vineyard plots separate throughout the initial winemaking process, and they may even do the same with grapes from sub-plots where clones or rootstocks are different.

This diversity of raw material, extended still further by varied pressing approaches and the choice of yeasts, gives a wonderfully broad palette from which to create sparkling wine. Frequently there are twenty-plus elements available to blend into the final wine, and sometimes that number stretches to one hundred or more. It takes formidable skill to foresee how a finished wine will taste. To increase the complexity of future

Components of the future sparkling wine lined up for blending at Rathfinny. RATHFINNY WINE ESTATE

vintage sparkling wines, or to contribute to the consistency of non-vintage cuvées, some of each year's base wines will be stored away as reserve wine, while reserve wine from earlier years will go into the new blend.

The next step is to get the blended wine fermenting again. The original fermentation agents of sugar and yeast have gone, so more have to be added, mixed with a small quantity of wine, as *liqueur de tirage*. The wine, now in crown-capped bottles strong enough to support the increasing pressure exerted by the liquid, is left for the second fermentation to occur. As that happens, there is no escape for the resulting bubbles of carbon dioxide, so sparkling wine is created, its alcohol level slightly higher than that of the base wine. Inside the bottle is a new residue of dead yeast cells (lees). This needs to be removed, though not immediately – the longer a wine remains in contact with the lees, the more complex its flavours, the result of a chemical process known as 'autolysis'. Those flavours often have hints of a bakery – brioche, perhaps, or toast – and the mouthfeel of the wine is also improved. For champagne, the minimum time resting on its lees in cool cellars is fifteen months; for many of the best sparkling wines, English as well as French, this stage extends for upwards of three years.

When the moment for the clean-up arrives, tradition and modernity combine. For centuries, the champagne technique – known as 'riddling' – was to place the bottles in angled holes in a wooden rack, neck pointing down. Each day, a skilled cellar hand gently shook each bottle and twisted it a few degrees, encouraging the sediment to settle in the neck. This continued until the bottle was fully inverted and all sediment was lodged next to the cap. Today, electrically powered metal cages called gyropalettes do in a few hours what took the cellar hand a month or more. Most UK sparkling wine wineries are equipped with gyropalettes, although, like all sparkling wine kit, they're expensive.

Now for the exciting part – getting rid of that lump of sediment. Most wineries dunk the neck of the bottle into a bath of glycol and water at a temperature of minus 20 to minus 25 degrees celsius, which freezes the top few centimetres of the bottle content. Once the bottle is upright again, the crown cap is removed and a

Disgorging bottles of English sparkling wine at Hambledon Vineyard. HAMBLEDON VINEYARD

pellet of rubbish is ejected by the force of the bubbles. The skill lies in stopping too much wine following it. This process, known as 'disgorging', is mechanized in most wineries, and the necessary machine is yet another example of the many costs involved in producing sparkling wine. A few wineries manage the rubbish ejection without the need to freeze, but they are the exception.

And so to completing the bottling. There is a gap now at the top of the bottle, so a little fill-up is required, of the same blend of wine. Usually, sugar is also added (this is referred to as the 'dosage'), to create the precise style of wine the maker wants. Then, in goes a big fat cork, compressed into the bottle neck and held in place with the traditional wire cage.

A very tiny amount of the sparkling wine made in England follows a different method, a difference subtly shown in the title the French use for it. This is the méthode ancestrale, as opposed to the méthode traditionelle described above. There is a French name for the result, too – pétillant naturel. Its abbreviation, pet nat, is now widely used wherever this style of wine is made. Pet nat is becoming something of a cult worldwide among drinkers who favour wines made as much as possible as nature intended. The English contribution comes from organic producers, with Davenport and Albury the pioneers. What happens in this method is that the initial fermentation of the wine is stopped, by cooling, before all the sugar has been converted to alcohol. The wine is then bottled, and as its temperature rises back to normal cellar levels fermentation starts again, producing the bubbles in the bottle. The fizz is gentler than in the traditional method, the alcohol level is lower, there is usually a sediment remaining – some makers recommend shaking this back into the liquid before serving, for extra flavour – and the final wine is likely to be a little sweeter, with a distinctive apple-y character. Pet nat is cheaper to make than traditional-method bottle-fermented wine, but is much more tricky to get right, and quite what the result will be with each batch is hard to predict exactly. When it turns out well it is fun to drink, especially as a lunchtime wine.

Making any sparkling wine certainly doesn't come cheap in the UK, and that is not down solely to the

Pet nat made at Albury Organic Vineyard by Monty Waldin.
ALBURY ORGANIC VINEYARD

or other appropriate material, and stick on the label. Wineries worldwide are inordinately proud of their bottling lines, which are boring in the extreme once you've seen one, two, maybe three. But there is some interesting technology around, so keep your eyes and ears open even when you're confronted with bottling lines four, five and more. I was glad I did that at Chapel Down, to learn of the use of lasers to ensure the labels and foils are correctly aligned.

At this point, there is another important aspect if the finished product is to be a commercial success: how the bottle looks. English wine for many years went rather too far down the route of over-complicated labels with frilly typefaces and fanciful designs. Some bottles still bear them, for nostalgia perhaps, or because consumers have grown so familiar with them. One example is Biddenden's ortega, which is a wine that is far more modern than its label indicates. For small producers, redesign is a big addition to the budget, so change is often slow.

Many of the sparkling wines follow the champagne precedents of gold or silver foil and neat name-emphasizing label design. Among still wines there is much more variety, and some very attractive solutions. Albourne Estate has chosen stylish paintings of wildlife seen in or around the vineyards; at Lyme Bay an evocative landscape – by a Scottish artist, but well suited to represent England – has been neatly tweaked so different wines have individuality within a common style. And there are many others.

So much for what is on the outside of the bottle. The contents are what consumers most care about. How can someone with no experience of a particular style of wine or of an individual winery's product judge what to buy? Tasting is obviously the very best route to making a happy choice, and a large number of UK vineyards welcome the public and pour their wares for visitors, either free at the cellar door or at more structured paid-for tastings. There is more about such possibilities later in this book. Another way to choose is to look for medal stickers on bottles. UK vineyards are very keen on entering their wines in competitions, which are usually judged blind (the bottles are covered by

cost of the essential equipment. To put the difference in context, one comparison is particularly pertinent. Yields from UK vineyards over recent years have averaged approximately 20 hectolitres per hectare, though that might rise a little as more large, well-tended vineyards come into production. In Champagne, the average is 66 hectolitres per hectare. Turn those figures into a more understandable unit, the bottle, and the result is that, from the same area of vineyard, for each single bottle of English sparkling wine more than three will be made in Champagne.

Would you buy this bottle?

Whatever type of wine is being made, the final stage is to put it into a bottle, cover the cork with a cap of foil

Wildlife at Albourne Estate appears on bottle labels. ALBOURNE ESTATE

Wine Awards, with a broader base of expert judges and an intention to provide a much more publicly visible showcase of the quality now achieved by the industry. The 293 entries in the first edition of the new competition were split roughly 60:40 in favour of still wines, but sparkling wines took 75 per cent of the gold medals.

The overall supreme champion award went to one of the latter, Coates & Seely La Perfide Blanc de Blancs 2009, from chardonnay grown on Hampshire chalk. At £65 a bottle, La Perfide is in the top price bracket of English sparkling wine, but the judges were effusive: 'Fabulously elegant and refined with the seductive toasted brioche and honey notes of age.' Nicholas Coates and Christian Seely must have been smiling broadly at the awards announcement: not just top wine, but also two more trophies for that same La Perfide blanc de blancs, plus another for La Perfide rosé 2009. Bolney Wine Estate (pinot gris), Lyme Bay Winery (bacchus) and Digby Fine English (classic cuvée) carried off the remaining trophies. Bolney was also named winery of the year.

Important as it is, that event is an insular one. Much, much broader in scope are the two principal competitions held in England, the International Wine Challenge and the Decanter World Wine Awards, where UK wines are judged against thousands of their peers worldwide (and can beat them, as Winbirri's Bacchus 2015 proved,

Christian Seely and just one of La Perfide's trophies at the inaugural UK Wine Awards. TOM GOLD PHOTOGRAPHY/WINEGB

anonymous wrappings so the judges make unprejudiced decisions). Some competitions are small and very local, others are big and international.

The UK regional wine associations hold annual contests, rewarding the different categories of wine made by their members. In 2017 the long-running umbrella event, the English and Welsh Wine of the Year Competition, was revamped to become the UK

by taking the latter event's 2017 award for best-value white wine from a single grape variety from any wine-making nation). The judges are as international as the entrant wines and offer experience of every aspect of the wine industry.

Some people in the trade are dismissive of the worth of the medals awarded in these and other wine competitions, arguing that such events are more commercial money-making exercises than true reflections of wine quality. Not so, I believe, certainly as far as the best are concerned. I judged for many years in the International Wine Challenge and I retain a very great respect for the rigour of the selection process. The Decanter awards, though run in a slightly different way, are equally professional. There is an issue at the lower levels of recognition, with the tag of 'commended' or a bronze medal. Sometimes, these can be awarded because the wines are rather better than those that aren't recognized at all, not because the bottles concerned have outstanding qualities in themselves. But it can be the case that great wines don't win higher awards because they are simply too quirky. Move up to silver or gold, however, and the wines should be special.

Beyond the UK-based competitions there are scores more, some more worthy of respect than others. Full results of most are available online, so a quick look will give an idea of the level of wines entered and hint at the value to be placed on the medals awarded. But

Bottles lined up before judging at the International Wine Challenge. AUTHOR

it can be difficult to understand why a wine may be awarded a gold medal in one competition yet only a bronze in another. The individual tastes of even the most punctilious of judges can play a part, or there might be a difference in the criteria of judging. The stage of the moon could even be a factor – there are serious proponents of the theory that the lunar calendar can have a significant effect on how wine tastes. And wine is a natural product. However high the quality standards of producers are, individual bottles can differ.

Consultant Stephen Skelton is an advocate of competition both in these wine-against-wine events and on a broader scale: 'It helps spur winemakers to higher things.' Overall, he agrees that quality has improved, but argues that older efforts certainly should not be dismissed out of hand. 'Sure, there were a lot of terrible wines in the past and the number of terrible wines is much, much lower now (although still not low enough). The best wines in the 1980s and 1990s were very good.'

Julia Trustram Eve, marketing director of WineGB, agrees that the late-twentieth-century past must not be forgotten in celebration of the present and future. 'One thing that is so special about the UK wine industry is the people who have been stalwarts for so long. They are still there, though they may be producing very different wines.'

Advice that has stood the test of time

Before we move entirely away from the subject of making wine, I can't resist offering a little more history, from John Evelyn's account of how it should be done, first published in 1669 and entitled *The Vintage*. This is thought to be the oldest description originally written in English (as opposed to being translated from another language) of the recommended process.

His very first advice is to 'gather your Grapes when very plump, and transparent'. Wine grapes can never be over-ripe, he contends, noting that 'where they make the best Wines, the Clusters hang till they are almost wasted'. As for pressing, 'in most places they tread them with their naked Feet in a Vat, pierced full of holes',

JOANNES EVELYN ARMIG.
REG. SOCIETATIS SOC.

John Evelyn, by Godfrey Kneller. WELLCOME LIBRARY, LONDON

though there are the alternative methods of heaping so many grapes into the vat 'that the very weight of the Bunches press themselves' or crushing them in 'an Engine like a Cider-press'. So what's new now?

Some of Evelyn's other instructions also have a very modern ring. For red wine, he advises leaving the juice with the skins 'till the tincture be to your liking'; he notes 'yet even Red Grapes will make a White-wine, if timely freed of the Hulk'; he describes the practice of rolling 'Casks about the Cellar to blend with the Lees', to be followed a few days later by racking off the wine 'with great improvement'. There is, too, mention of the use of wood chips (which is frequent now – though not a UK practice – as a cheaper means of giving wines something of the character that comes from barrel fermentation or maturation). But in Evelyn's day the wood was green beech, not dry oak, and the chips were used for clarifying the wine, not flavouring it.

As with much else in the story of English wine, what is current so often reflects historic practice.

Chapter 6

Meet the Late Twentieth-Century Pioneers, the People behind England's Appearance on the World Wine Map

WHEN MODERN ENGLISH WINE'S HOLY TRINITY, Raymond Barrington Brock, Edward Hyams and George Ordish, laid down the creed for a future industry, they needed disciples. The first appeared in the somewhat unlikely form of a man with a distinguished military and diplomatic service career. Major-General Sir Guy Salisbury-Jones fought in the two world wars – winning the Military Cross in the first and in the second, after time in Egypt and Greece, serving in the team that planned the Normandy landings – and afterwards became Marshal of the Diplomatic Service. He loved all things French, had friends at the champagne house Pol Roger, and happened, in his retirement, to live in a house set on Hampshire's vine-friendly chalk.

One brief event in that military career was, decades later, to prompt the ending of what could be argued had been the first true break in largish-scale wine production in the UK since Roman times. The planting of England's first modern commercial vineyard was, Sir Guy said in an address to the Royal Society of Arts in 1973, all down to a moment in the cold and muddy autumn of 1917, when French soldiers sharing a trench with the British guardsmen poured beakers of wine for their allies. The gesture, he continued, 'consolidated my love, not only for France, but [also] for her wine'.

Thirty-four years after that morale-boosting encounter in the trenches, as Sir Guy looked down the sunny slope stretching below his house at Hambledon in Hampshire and pondered how best to use the land, his stepson put forward the 'wild suggestion' of planting vines. Soon, following meetings with Hyams and Brock, the wild suggestion was on the way to becoming reality. With his gardener, Mr Blackman – 'without whom I could have achieved nothing' – Sir Guy set off to the vineyards of Burgundy. Part of the entertainment was a banquet given by the Confrérie des Chevaliers du Tastevin, in the iconic fine-wine location of the former Cistercian monastery of Clos Vougeot. 'I have often thought since that it was under the influence of Burgundian hospitality that I ordered four thousand vines,' he told his 1973 RSA audience.

Those vines were mainly seyval blanc, recommended then although regarded with mixed feelings now, plus a little chardonnay and pinot noir. They were planted early in 1952, and the first wine was on sale three years later. It was the beginning of England's nascent new industry.

A wine with noble qualities

Given the lack of experience of commercial wine production in England at the time, the difficulties of the climate, the singularity of the principal variety chosen and the lack of an established market for the local product, Hambledon proved remarkably successful. Sir Guy was modest about his wine, though he acknowledged at the RSA lecture that the results had improved with time and added experience. 'At the outset our wine may have been a little frivolous, but since then it has acquired more noble qualities.' One Frenchman who tasted it likened it to still champagne, it was listed at a major London restaurant and sold through the

Milldown House, the home of Sir Guy Salisbury-Jones, and the modern vineyard. CHRIS DIXON PHOTOGRAPHY/HAMBLEDON VINEYARD

Peter Dominic retail chain. It also travelled further afield. Sir Guy's wines 'were served on the QE2, in British Embassies around the world, in the Houses of Parliament and in export markets around the world including the USA and Japan', the website of the present Hambledon Vineyard proudly declares. They were on the menu in 1972 for a dinner that Queen Elizabeth II planned in Paris for President Georges Pompidou, but the arrangements were almost thwarted when French customs refused the import on the grounds that there was 'no such thing as English wine'. Release of the bottles was secured only as a result of some very straight talking to the customs official by Steven Spurrier, then a wine merchant in Paris. (Spurrier's career continued as a distinguished wine writer and consultant, and he celebrated fifty years in wine by creating his own sparkling wine vineyard; *see* Chapter 7 for more on that venture.)

Guy Salisbury-Jones tried hard to show to potential followers the effort involved in setting up a new vineyard, admitting he had 'given little serious thought to the endless problems involved in viticulture' when he planted his own vines. He also spelled out, in detail, the cost. In the early 1970s, to plant a vineyard of 1.2 hectares, the smallest viable size, on already-owned land and create a winery and cellar in existing buildings would mean an investment of some £15,600. Today,

the equivalent outlay would leave little change out of £225,000 – and that was for a winery far smaller and equipment much less sophisticated than at twenty-first-century English wine estates. Sir Guy himself surely spent more, for his vineyard was half as big again.

Sir Guy Salisbury-Jones (wearing jacket) with Mr Blackman, friends and family. HAMBLEDON VINEYARD

With the help from 1966 of his manager and winemaker Bill Carcary, he continued to produce wine until his death in 1985. It was very much a family-and-friends operation, as an evocative Pathe film of the 1971 harvest shows, with the grapes being picked into wooden baskets, emptied into barrels, and then crushed by Mr Blackman in something that looks like an oversized mincing machine. The filmmakers remarked on how good the vineyard looked, but had severe doubts over the quality of the end product, commenting that 'the grapes are too small and too green' and the pressed juice 'does not look attractive at all'. They may well have been too pessimistic. The 1969 vintage had been much lauded, described by one enthusiast as lying between 'a delicate dry Vouvray and a first-class crisp Moselle', and with another identifying a 'sweet waft of English flowers'.

Sir Guy's influence extended far beyond the small village of Hambledon, which probably remains best known not for wine but as the home of modern English cricket. He was founder president of the English Vineyards Association and worked intensively both to establish recognition among British consumers of the new wines being made on their doorstep and, behind the public scenes, to reduce the duty burden on them – a task still faced by his successors.

Hambledon wine continued in the hands of the vineyard's next owner, John Patterson, for some years more, with further plantings and improved winemaking and storage facilities. By the early 1990s, after Patterson's death, the few remaining rows of vines were unloved and their crop unappealing – until a saviour appeared, in the form of Yorkshireman Ian Kellett. The story of his revival of Hambledon Vineyard as a leading producer of sparkling wine is told later in this book.

Something similar to the Salisbury-Jones initiative happened a little further south-west in Hampshire, at the third commercial vineyard of the 1950s. This had a far, far older history – it was that thirteenth-century monastic vineyard where King John suggested the abbot should send to France for something better. Margaret Gore-Browne and her rather less vineyard-enthusiastic husband had spent much of their married

life in Africa. Back home in the late 1950s, they moved into a large house – fortuitously named The Vineyards – on the edge of the Beaulieu estate, and revived the land's vinous history, planting mostly müller-thurgau and seyval blanc, plus a few red varieties, and building their winery. They also gained some notoriety for their increasingly ingenious efforts to rid the vineyard of grape-consuming blackbirds and thrushes. A family of young sparrowhawks, raised in a laundry basket and initially fed on dead day-old baby chicks from the kitchen freezer, was one quite successful solution. The enterprise continued for some fifteen years, and Margaret Gore-Browne's contribution to the growth of English and, notably, Welsh wine is remembered in the resplendent Gore-Browne trophy she donated in her husband's memory, which is awarded to the best wine in the annual UK competition. In the mid-1970s the vineyard passed into the hands of the Montagu family

The Gore-Browne trophy. TOM GOLD PHOTOGRAPHY/WINEGB

and has remained as a small feature of the modern Beaulieu estate.

Between the start of Hambledon and that of Beaulieu there had been another pioneer, Jack Ward. With a friend, Ian Howie, he had founded the Merrydown cider and fruit wine business at Horam in East Sussex in 1946. In 1954, he moved into real wine, planting a little under a hectare with an assortment of grape varieties. He'd hardly had time to establish them properly when it was decided to sell the vineyard for development. Ward persevered, planting again. The two sites available were far from ideal, the heavy soil of one – a former brickworks – requiring major drainage work and composting effort before vines could produce even small crops.

A co-operative approach to put wine on shop shelves

Alongside the company's own vineyards, there was a more important development for English wine – the Merrydown Co-operative Scheme. More and more small vineyards had been planted in the 1960s, and Ward realized that supporting these was the best thing he could do to promote the product that so enthused him. He set up a contract winemaking operation, with a co-operative, non-profit-making rationale. Growers handed over their grapes and either paid the full cost of turning them into wine or received a proportion of the final product, with the remainder retained by Merrydown to turn into a blended wine sold under a single label. It was exactly what the new industry needed, and a high proportion of England's growers with grapes to harvest took advantage of it – including Princess Margaret, whose few bunches of fruit came from wall-trained vines at Kensington Palace.

In *The Wines of Britain and Ireland*, Stephen Skelton was enthusiastic: 'At a time when good equipment and technical knowledge were both in short supply, it had certainly enabled many vineyards to get a properly made and presented commercial product on the shelf.' But, as English vineyards grew in size and their vines matured, producing larger crops, more of them moved away from the co-operative scheme to set up their own wineries. Commercial considerations prevailed and by 1980 all Merrydown grape wine operations, contracting as well as growing, were abandoned.

What of these larger 1960s and 1970s vineyards now? Many are names only in England's vinous history. But one that flourished, and where control has moved on to generations two and three of the family, is Biddenden Vineyards, close to Ashford, the oldest in Kent and one of the longest-established anywhere in England. It came about, remarkably, because of a BBC Radio *Woman's Hour* broadcast. Richard and Joyce Barnes owned an apple farm, and the late 1960s were a bad time for growers of traditional English varieties, with the burgeoning supermarkets demanding granny smith and golden delicious rather than cox or russet. The effect was felt even in cidermaking, which was Biddenden's speciality. Wine grapes, suggested the speaker on that 1967 radio programme, might be an alternative for the apple growers, for the required growing conditions of the two were comparatively similar.

Joyce Barnes listened with interest and broached the subject with her husband. Soon, Richard Barnes was off on an exploratory trip to Europe (no internet then for instant research) and in 1969 the first Biddenden vines were planted, the plot a tiny forerunner of the present 9 hectares. Given the advice of the time, the early choice was largely germanic varieties – but not entirely. Tucked behind the winery, whose tanks peek over the top of the plot, are two rows of venerable pinot noir vines, planted in 1972. Tom Barnes, Richard's grandson, couldn't tell me whether they were the oldest examples of the variety surviving in England, but he suspected there could be few challengers. They remain generously productive and the family have no plans to grub them up in favour of new vines; they will simply fill in the gaps as the least-sturdy elders reach the end of their life.

Across the sheltered valley from the pinot noir, the major variety – occupying just over half of the total vineyard area – is ortega, which also dates back to the early days of Biddenden's involvement in wine. It flourishes on the sandy loam-over-clay soil, surviving

Pinot noir planted at Biddenden Vineyards in 1972. AUTHOR

bad weather, appears in bottle in near-dry and off-dry versions and has brought a number of respected awards to the Barnes' display shelf. Why, says marketing manager Victoria Rose, abandon a vine which has such happy results?

The ortega has compatriots in the vineyard. Reichensteiner and scheurebe, with pinot noir, are the components of a traditional-method sparkling

Ortega, major variety at Biddenden Vineyards. BIDDENDEN VINEYARDS

white, bacchus provides an aromatic dry white and two more still wines come from dornfelder, a light red and a medium-dry rosé. But among the total of eleven varieties now planted are others that are a much less conventional sight in England. Gamay is made into a rosé sparkler, and gewürztraminer is being trialled.

Biddenden may have a lengthy history, but the estate's insistence on quality and consistency is very modern. That approach should be obligatory for every vineyard in the UK, Rose believes. Given how many drinkers are still unfamiliar with the home product, if they encounter a bad example they won't condemn only that individual wine, she warns: 'They will say English wine is terrible, full stop.'

Next, a very different approach

The direction taken by another crucial pioneer husband-and-wife team in modern English wine was radically dissimilar to Biddenden's largely germanic approach – although by the time their first vines went into the ground almost two decades had passed since the Barnes' first plantings. It wasn't just the vine choice; the individuals involved could hardly have been more different.

Stuart and Sandy Moss hailed from Chicago. They were both successful business people, he in the manufacture of medical equipment, she as an antiques dealer, and they had travelled frequently to England. By the early 1980s, they were looking for an idyllic retirement home, and Sandy Moss had an ambition to become involved in wine. 'All I ever wanted was a small English house, two acres of vines, my spinning wheel and a never-ending bottle of port,' she told a *Daily Telegraph* journalist five years after the release of their first wine. That wine started what was to become a relentless haul of trophies and medals. 'We never expected to do things on this scale,' she added.

When they saw Nyetimber, a medieval gem that Henry VIII had gifted to Anne of Cleves, the first part of Sandy's dream was achieved, though 'small' is hardly the adjective most people would use to describe the half-timbered manor house with its terraced gardens,

pools and 40-plus hectares of land. First mention of the estate – then medium-sized and home to nineteen families – came in Domesday Book, and it is surely appropriate that a highly significant modern change should have happened precisely nine hundred years later. In 1986 the Mosses became the new owners of Nyetimber, and two years later they planted their first vines. Not the germanic favourites: no, the Mosses had haughtier aims. They wanted to make sparkling wine to match the quality of the world's best. They turned for advice and practical help to Kit Lindlar, who was then essentially England's lone specialist consultant on bottle-fermented sparkling wine and had been influential in persuading a number of small growers in Kent towards the champagne grape varieties. As a result, the vines set into Nyetimber's greensand-based soil were the classics of French fizz, chardonnay, pinot noir and pinot meunier. More than that, the equipment to turn their grapes into wine, and more advice, came from Champagne.

There was profound scepticism from many, but not all, leading figures in the UK industry, which was then almost entirely focused on still wines. Around the same time, Chris Foss had initiated the first wine courses at Plumpton College, an hour's drive further east in Sussex. Foss, a microbiologist by training, came from a sound wine background – a family vineyard in Bordeaux, which he had run until the decision to sell up brought him back to the UK and, given the paucity of winemaking opportunities, a teacher-training course. He was offered a job managing Horam vineyard, but his income would have been peanuts, even compared with a teacher's salary. Then came the Plumpton possibility. As the thirty-year anniversary of his employment there approached, he recalled how it all began: 'I went along to the college. They said, here's a desk, let's have some wine courses, you start in September.' The space provided was less than ideal for teaching a subject in which appreciating aromas was important. 'The wine centre was in the poultry area, an unused shed. It was difficult tasting – everything still smelled of chicken.'

During the first year, Foss organized a field trip to Champagne. Why, he wondered, wasn't there more

A place to achieve high aspirations: Nyetimber. AUTHOR

interest in the region among those making wine in the UK? It was the nearest established wine area, and in many ways the most similar in terms of soil and climate. England, he believed, should be making sparkling wine, even though he wasn't optimistic then that champagne grapes would ripen – 'chardonnay berries were like frozen peas'.

The students on the trip were enthusiastic and a masterclass in Sussex with a champagne oenologist followed, with Stuart and Sandy Moss in attendance. Sandy, by then enrolled at Plumpton, asked Foss for help to find further expert support as she began her new

career in winemaking. The choice was Jean-Manuel Jacquinot. For Foss, Jacquinot is 'the unsung hero of English sparkling wine', with an invaluable consultancy role in many more early ventures into English fizz. All

Chris Foss in the Plumpton College winery: England should be making sparkling wine. IAN PACK/PLUMPTON COLLEGE

his professional experience apart, the Frenchman had the essential qualification of speaking the language of those he mentored, learned by working in a vineyard in Poonah owned by the father of a Plumpton student.

At Nyetimber the vines flourished; from 1989 to 1991 more land was planted, bringing the total vineyard area to some 16 hectares, remarkably large by the standards of the time; and by 1992 there were sufficient grapes for a first vintage to be made by Sandy Moss, with Jacquinot looking over her shoulder. Stuart Moss took responsibility for marketing.

Plenty of today's most serious producers of English sparkling wine turn some of the grapes they pick in the first few years into still wine, so that its release the year following harvest can bring at least some income to set against the massive initial investment. The Mosses didn't go down that route; instead, they made their entire crop into sparkling wine and left it gently maturing until they believed it was ready to drink. The reaction in 1997, when that 1992 all-chardonnay blanc de blancs was released, was awe and astonishment. 'The collective crashing of jaws to the floor could be heard in London when the wine came top of a blind tasting of sparkling wines in Paris – yes, Paris, France,' wrote that same *Telegraph* journalist.

A more measured comment comes from Stephen Skelton, on his English sparkling wine website: 'Suddenly, everyone woke up to the fact that good wine, even stunningly good wine, could be made from hitherto seemingly unworkable varieties – chardonnay, pinot noir and pinot meunier – and what was more, the wine could be sold at a premium price.' Skelton admits he had been sceptical when he first heard of the Mosses' plans and, even after those first medals, in his 2001 *The Wines of Britain and Ireland*, he described chardonnay as a grape 'for the brave and patient'. A few more years changed his view. 'As a variety for the UK, chardonnay appears to be more and more at home,' he wrote in his comprehensive *Wine Growing in Great Britain* (2014).

Nyetimber has gone from strength to strength, though its ownership has changed – the Mosses sold the estate in 2001 and returned to the States soon afterwards. English sparkling wine had moved on, said Stuart Moss, and his and Sandy's very personal approach needed to be replaced by something much more big-business-like. As it certainly has, at Nyetimber and at scores of other serious, professional estates. We'll meet more of the people concerned in the next chapter.

The alma mater of England's winemakers

At this point, it is worth looking more closely at what the wine centre at Plumpton College has achieved. 'There isn't anybody in English wine who hasn't been to Plumpton,' says Foss, with only a little exaggeration. The long list of names includes Mike Roberts and Owen Elias, as well as many of the younger generation now making multi-medal-winning English fizz.

From the original poultry shed, the department shifted to a much larger one, where there was the luxury of

Not the keys to the door, but to vine-growing and winemaking: Plumpton College student Sally MacGarry. PLUMPTON COLLEGE

water, refrigeration and considerably more equipment. A new, purpose-built centre came into use in 2006, with a £500,000 extension opened in 2014 by the Duchess of Cornwall; sponsors included Rathfinny (the Rathfinny Research Centre), Château de Sours and Merrydown (the Jack Ward Laboratory). Wine studies are tailored to students' needs, both in the hands-on growing of vines and turning their fruit into wine and in wine business management. A link with the University of Brighton has formalized the qualifications: there are foundation diplomas and degrees, BSc and BA honours degrees, a post-graduate masters programme, all available full-time or part-time. Short courses cover the principles of vine-growing and winemaking, while other sessions work towards the Wine and Spirit Education Trust diploma.

Government money helped with the introduction of the practical Wine Skills training programme for UK wine producers, providing day sessions and seminars on such subjects as vineyard sustainability, the safe use of pesticides and the business aspects of sparkling wine production. The original two rows of vines have gone, replaced by 8 hectares of commercial vineyard, producing 20,000 to 30,000 bottles a year from the champagne varieties and, as befits a research organization, a host more including the UK's biggest range of piwis, the new generation of disease-resistant vinifera vines. The wines are a commercial project, with still and sparkling styles, but buyers also have the chance to try students' state-of-the-art experiments, such as the college's first skin-contact white wine.

Post-graduate research activity continues to grow. 'We want to be the research hub for the industry, solving problems as well as educating,' says Foss, who has moved from being a one-man band to heading a staff of ten. So there is the pan-Europe project with the aim of developing viticultural techniques to face up to climate change, more locally related work on yeasts for second fermentation, development of a new bacterium for malolactic conversion, and much besides. The choice of nearby Brighton as the location for the 2016 International Cool-Climate Wine Symposium 'helped put us on the map' – an understatement indeed for an event that attracted 600 delegates from thirty

countries for three days of discussion on every aspect of making fine wine in cooler places and marketing the results.

Wine students come to Plumpton from all corners of the world and take back what they learn. This small English agricultural college is now internationally important.

This is also a good moment to look at the broader structure of the UK wine industry. Until the end of 2017 there were two central bodies, the United Kingdom Vineyards Association (UKVA) and English Wine Producers (EWP). The former was born out of the English Vineyards Association (EVA), set up in 1967 with Sir Guy Salisbury-Jones and Jack Ward as its inaugural president and chairman respectively. Despite a limited budget, the EVA did all it could for its growing membership. It provided practical help through events and publications related to wine vine-growing, represented growers' and winemakers' interests in discussions with government bodies, promoted members' wine to consumers, introduced and implemented a pre-EU quality control scheme and further encouraged quality through the annual Wine of the Year competition. When it morphed into the UKVA in 1996, the organizational structure changed, but the association retained all elements of its support and advisory role for the people who grew the vines and made the wines.

The EWP was set up in 1993, its aim to raise the public profile of English and Welsh wines. It provided the answers to the media's questions about English wine, instigated such successful happenings as English Wine Week and the annual trade tasting, showed the wine-interested public how to find their way to the vineyards and wine-related events, and ensured the availability of a host of accessible online information, from the latest news of the industry to the places where wines could be bought.

In summer 2017, after lengthy discussions, members of the two bodies agreed to their merger, effective from 1 January 2018, a move that makes very good sense both for those in involved in producing the UK's wine and for those who enjoy drinking it. The new Wines of Great Britain Limited (WineGB) has taken over the roles of

A toast to the new single voice of the UK's wine industry:
Peter Gladwin (left) and Simon Robinson.

TOM GOLD PHOTOGRAPHY/WINEGB

the bodies it has united, but most crucially it provides a single, stronger voice for the industry and a clear vision for its future. The change is not abrupt: chosen as first chairman of WineGB was Simon Robinson of Hattingley Valley Wines, who immediately before had been chairman of EWP, with as his deputy Peter Gladwin of Nutbourne Vineyards, the last chairman of UKVA. WineGB, they said, will develop the strengths and skills of the two previous organizations, supporting vineyards large and small, as well as working to boost exports, attract investment and encourage wine tourism. 'We also have the opportunity to build a strong generic brand for our wines.' The noise about English wine isn't going to quieten for a long time yet.

Chapter 7

Sparkling Success: The Best Can Beat Champagne

'A FINER FLAVOUR THAN THE BEST CHAMPAIGN.'
Spelling apart, that is the perfect description for the best of English wine in the twenty-first century – except that those words were written more than 250 years ago. By contemporary accounts, the wine made by the Honourable Charles Hamilton at Painshill Park in Surrey did sparkle, but most historic descriptions of English wine refer to its similarity to a burgundian or rhenish style, not fizz.

The champagne-style bubbles began in earnest only late in the twentieth century, after Chicago emigrés

Stuart and Sandy Moss had bought the Tudor manor of Nyetimber in West Sussex and set about realizing their ambition to make wine – not just any wine, but one that would be the equal of the most prestigious fizz in the world. In 1998, exactly ten years after the first vines of the noble varieties from which champagne is made were planted, their newly released second vintage – 1993 – was declared the best sparkling wine in the world by judges in one of the biggest international wine competitions.

The Mosses' wine was not to be alone at the top for

Ridgeview vines stretching towards the South Downs. RIDGEVIEW ESTATE

long. In 1995, before Nyetimber made world headlines, Mike and Chris Roberts had invested the proceeds of the sale of their computer business in land for vine-growing some 30 kilometres eastwards along the same geological formation. With advice from Kit Lindlar, they also planted the champagne big three, chardonnay, pinot noir and pinot meunier. Ridgeview Estate soon joined the medal laureates.

It was the beginning of what is now the major focus of English wine. By 2015 an estimated two-thirds of the UK's average annual production of 5 million bottles was sparkling wine. As more and more of the new English vineyards, most of them concentrating on classic bottle-fermented sparkling wine from the three champagne grape varieties, come into full production, and the bottle total soars to 10 million and above, that proportion is rising. Hugh Liddell, owner of one of those newer vineyards, Cottonworth in Hampshire, cheerfully sums up the situation: 'The fun has just started!'

There is clearly a big market for fizz in the UK – after the French, Britons drink more bottles of champagne than anyone else. So having a home-grown alternative of similar quality at comparable or even slightly lower prices is good news for patriotic buyers.

Two Renaissance men who made all this possible

Those buyers should raise a glass to celebrate far older British involvement with bubbly wine – way back before the first vintage of Nyetimber, before the first commercial quantity of traditional-method English sparkling wine was produced from the Carr Taylors' unexpectedly large 1983 crop of reichensteiner, before Raymond Barrington Brock made the first twentieth-century experimental UK bottle-fermented wine, even before Charles Hamilton's 'champaign'. In 1662 Dr Christopher Merret, a Gloucester-born physician, scientist and writer, presented a paper to the Royal Society detailing how wine was deliberately made 'brisk and sparkling' by the addition of 'vast quantities of sugar and molasses'. In essence, this was the secondary fermentation-in-bottle technique popularly attributed to Dom Pérignon, described six years before he began his winemaking career at the abbey of Hautvillers. Rather than create bubbles, the monk was in fact more concerned to rid the wine of them.

Written explanation of liquid technique apart, there was practical input too. It was a Briton who invented a bottle that could safely contain that brisk and sparkling drink, avoiding the all-too-frequent explosions of weaker examples. That inventor was Kenelm Digby, a seventeenth-century man of many parts – courtier, diplomat, philosopher, astrologer, alchemist, cookbook author, even privateer. Alongside all those activities he also owned a glassworks where wine bottles were produced in the 1630s. They were a cut above the norm of the time, made from a high-sand-content mix melted in an exceptionally hot furnace. The result was strong enough to withstand high interior pressure, whether from deliberate in-bottle fermentation or from naturally re-fermenting wine. The bottles even looked

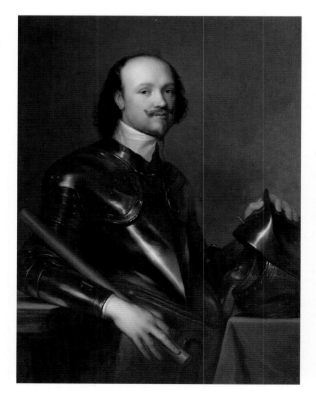

An anonymous portrait of Sir Kenelm Digby.

the part, featuring a punt, the deep indentation in the base that is characteristic of modern sparkling wine bottles. Rivals attempted to claim Digby's glory, but Parliament confirmed the invention was his alone.

If sparkling wine was poured from English seventeenth-century bottles, the original liquid probably wasn't made in England. Historical sources suggest much came from Champagne as still wine and was modified here as Christopher Merret described. One significant importer is believed to have been Charles de Marguetel de Saint Denis de Saint-Evremond, a distinguished soldier, writer and wine lover who got into political and military trouble in France. He fled across the Channel, where he (and the still wine from Champagne that he brought with him) became a favourite of Charles II. The king rewarded him by appointing him governor of the duck islands in St James's Park in London, a strange post, but one that gave its holder a considerable income and prestige.

To complete the biography, when Saint-Evremond died aged 90-plus, he was buried in Westminster Abbey, his monument in Poets' Corner close to that of Shakespeare. And he retains a connection to modern English sparkling wine: he is commemorated in the name of the first estate to be set up in England by a champagne house, Taittinger's Domaine Evremond.

Building on the pioneering base

And that leads, very suitably, to names already big in the home business. First, an update on Nyetimber. The Mosses' immediate successor was pop song writer and producer Andy Hill, but in 2006 he sold the Sussex estate, for a reported £7.4 million, to Dutch-born lawyer and entrepreneur Eric Heerema. A man with immense bubbly ambition, he was ready to build on what had led to the 'incredible thriving industry' of English sparkling wine, on a far larger, far more commercial scale. That 'thriving' description comes from the head winemaker Heerema chose to make it happen, Cherie Spriggs. A Canadian/UK national, Spriggs and her husband Brad Greatrix, both with considerable experience, wanted

Cherie Spriggs, head winemaker at Nyetimber. NYETIMBER

to move together to a new wine challenge. They had heard of Heerema's plans and made a direct approach. Happily for both sides, it all fell into place and in 2007 Spriggs was appointed to head the winemaking, with Greatrix working alongside her.

From the Mosses' 16 hectares, the estate has expanded to more than 170. There are five vineyards in Sussex: two at Nyetimber itself and three at Tillington, a short distance to the north-west – all on greensand – and two on Hampshire chalk near Stockbridge, an 80-minute drive away. The winemaking has been moved from the estate to a purpose-built facility in Crawley, where access is much easier than through the narrow lanes around Nyetimber, and one of the barns overlooking the house and immediate grounds has been converted to an impressive reception area, though general wine tourism wasn't on the immediate agenda, Spriggs told me in spring 2017.

But why are the wines special? Spriggs argues that choice of soil is important, reflecting in the taste of the wine. 'Without question there are clear differences between the chalk and greensand,' she says. 'The beauty of greensand is the wonderful brightness of fruit it gives. The flavours are clear and really bright. When you grow vines on chalk soil the way acid is perceived is different. It is perceived earlier, up front, and the overall impression is of acidity being lower: there is no shock of acidity at end.' Within the vineyards on the same soils the differences from one parcel of vines to another are far subtler, she continues, and understanding all the effects is a continuing learning process. But having such a variety of raw materials for the wines is invaluable – fruit from each of the seventy-five parcels of vines, and from each of the sub-blocks within those, is pressed and fermented separately. The vines themselves can add additional elements: for example, she notes that 'something special' comes from the 30-year-old chardonnay plot close to the house. It is because of that, rather than for any feelings of nostalgia for the early days of Nyetimber's wine, that those vines escaped replacement by more productive youngsters.

Cherie Spriggs has put her own mark on the wines, with the aim of making them more appealing. Some commentators use the word 'feminine', which she takes 'as a compliment'. From the beginning she was adamant on the importance of quality control. Also, she puts almost all of Nyetimber's wine through malolactic conversion, except in the very ripest years. 'Every wine country in the world has an Achilles heel. Perhaps in England it is too much acidity. Why not use malo? It's a wonderful non-invasive way to soften acidity.' Winemakers must always remember, she says firmly, that they are creating something that should give pleasure, and there must be balance and harmony in their wines.

Despite Nyetimber's importance in proving the world-beating quality of English sparkling wine, the estate can't sit back on its laurels, Spriggs insists. Key to winemaking success is to evaluate the available fruit and decide how to turn it into the best possible wine. It's demanding, she says. 'This is the hardest job I have ever had – I love it.' Heerema is closely involved in all that goes on and he knew from the outset that his investment would not be for short-term gain but for long-term progress. 'He doesn't think in years, he thinks in generations,' says Spriggs. His children are too young to be thinking of future career paths, but might this be the start of a wine dynasty of very unusual national origin (Heerema's wife is Scottish)?

England's first sparkling wine dynasty

It certainly wouldn't be the first example of England's sparkling wine industry spanning more than a single generation. At Ridgeview, which followed hard on the heels of Nyetimber and has a similarly impressive haul of gold and silver ware, the next generation's commitment is complete. The English wine world went into deep mourning when Ridgeview founder Mike Roberts died in 2014. He was a much-loved figure, ready with advice and help to all those with bubbling ambitions, and his name is still on many lips. But Ridgeview remains the Roberts family business. Son Simon is the winemaker, daughter Tamara is the CEO and daughter-in-law Mardi is in charge of marketing. They cherish and celebrate that family ethos.

Over the quarter-century since the first vines went into the clay-with-limestone soil looking south towards Sussex landmark Ditchling Beacon on the South Downs, the business has expanded hugely. Now the 7-hectare vineyard at Ridgeview itself provides only a small part of the fruit that goes into present bottles;

Ready to walk the greensand: boots at Nyetimber. AUTHOR

The Roberts family, with Chris and Mike in the centre. RIDGEVIEW ESTATE

grapes are sourced from a further 50 hectares of vines owned by partnership growers. The biggest of those partners is Tinwood, 45 kilometres to the west at the base of the downs, which has a 25 per cent share in the business, a co-operation that works well for both parties. It's not just the broad sourcing of fruit that sets Ridgeview apart from many other, more self-contained producers of sparkling wine. It also makes wine under their own labels for customers such as Marks & Spencer and Laithwaite's, and it keeps its winery equipment in efficient use by contract winemaking for other growers, either direct from their grapes or by completing the complexities of turning their still wine into fizz. Much credit is due to Ridgeview for putting English sparkling wine into the glasses – and smiles on to the faces – of so many new consumers. Also, via placements from nearby Plumpton College, the Roberts family have helped to train many of the winemakers now in charge of England's leading sparkling wine cellars. Mike Roberts' legacy is his

family's continuing and very special contribution to what he loved so much.

From the beginning, the family were determined to get it right. Vine clones, winery equipment, yeasts for first and second fermentations, winemaking advice: all followed the champagne lead. Given the similarities between the two regions, it was so logical for southern England's wine producers to go down that same route, Mike Roberts argued. The scale was small initially, with expansion at a pace that the business could support. The latest advance has been a second winery, ready for the 2018 harvest and almost doubling production capacity, to a potential approaching 500,000 bottles a year. And with the steady, sensible progress has come the opportunity to hold back wines to increase the reserve stock, to move from vintage to non-vintage (NV) for the signature range. The change happened early in 2017 for chardonnay-led Bloomsbury, followed soon afterwards by Cavendish traditional blend and Fitzrovia rosé. Their capital-themed names are Mike

At Rathfinny, you can see the sea. VIV BLAKEY/RATHFINNY WINE ESTATE

Roberts' tribute to Christopher Merret, who practised in London, with Fitzrovia included because Roberts' office had been located there. The NV wines are in no way radically different from their vintage predecessors: the move is all about consistency and assuring a style that is familiar to drinkers, year on year, exactly as the big champagne houses do. But there will still be vintage individuality in the top-end wines, for the best of both worlds.

Like her father-in-law, Mardi Roberts is adamant that the terroir argument in English sparkling wine stretches far beyond whether or not vines are planted on pure chalk soil. 'We see terroir as a bit of everything – climate, soil, talent of viticulture and winemaking.' Diversity in the raw material is to be celebrated, as is the increasing number of growers who produce fine wine, she says. Informing potential consumers is vital, too, and wine tourism is important in achieving that. Cellar-door visitors at Ridgeview have been doubling year on year and they are drawn because of the quality of the wine, not by add-on attractions. This is how great English sparkling wine began, and will continue.

The very highest of ambitions

Alongside the familiar names, many new ones are emerging. The most audacious of all recent vineyard initiatives is that of Rathfinny Wine Estate, set high on the South Downs above the picture-postcard East Sussex village of Alfriston. The ambition of owners Mark and Sarah Driver can be summed up in a single four-letter word: huge. The estate itself stretches over almost 250 hectares, two-thirds of which are destined for vines, all due to be yielding close to capacity by 2023. And while at a good number of the vineyards in the far south of England you can almost smell the sea, here you can actually see it.

Rathfinny is some retirement project, but for Mark Driver retirement has come unusually early. After building a successful hedge fund management company he took the decision in 2010 to step back from high finance. He was forty-six and had no very clear plan of how to occupy himself, other than an intention to buy land. Entirely accidentally, when scanning the A–Z list of available university courses with his eldest daughter, he reached 'V' and found viticulture. 'I had no idea that you could study viticulture in England,' he told me. An idea was born – but English wine? 'I'd tasted it back in the eighties, and it was awful.' Perhaps things had changed, so he set up a blind tasting, comparing English sparkling wines with similarly priced champagnes. There would be no challenge, he thought. He found his francophile anticipation was entirely wrong, and his decision was made. Instead of looking for a non-specific estate, he moved to searching for one where he could grow grapes and create his own challenge to England's best fizz.

'I love wine, and in twenty-five years in the City, with a fair amount of entertaining, I got to drink some pretty special wines.' His own had to match them. As part of the new plan, he was determined to increase his knowledge, so he enrolled on the winemaking foundation degree course at Plumpton College. But before he had attended his first lecture he had become the owner of what looks set to be England's largest wine estate. The majestic South Downs site had become available while he was sailing – his and Sarah's hobby – in the Mediterranean: 'I looked on Google Earth and thought, this is wonderful.' The deal was done, and planning the estate's new role became course projects for Driver and

Sarah and Mark Driver among the Rathfinny vines. VIV BLAKEY/
RATHFINNY WINE ESTATE

fellow Plumpton students. Beyond that, the Drivers have become important supporters of the college's broader work, funding a research winery, opened in 2014, that brings the Rathfinny name to the wine students from around the world.

Buying an estate of that size, planting so many vines, building a state-of-the-art winery designed to cope comfortably when Rathfinny is at full 1-million-plus bottle production, plus associated work converting ruined barns into comfortable, bespoke-fitted accommodation for visitors and seasonal staff, planting some 10,000 trees, developing space for tours and events (Rathfinny is fast becoming a rather special wedding venue), and much more, doesn't come cheap. In spring 2017, with plenty still to do, Mark Driver was prepared to say only that his investment at that point had topped £10 million.

From the outset, the intention had been to create a fully commercial business: 'I don't want to do this as a hobby.' Rathfinny won't be perfect, he accepts. 'This is a completely new industry and we will make mistakes. But as long as we learn we will take the industry forward. We're looking to get more things right than things we get wrong.' One early mistake was to indulge his love of riesling and plant the variety. That didn't work. Though the grapes appeared ripe, 'we just didn't get the flavour'. In April 2017, chardonnay vines replaced the failed riesling.

The Drivers' confidence is infectious, but not everyone in the English sparkling wine industry is as sanguine about Rathfinny. The major question is whether vines will flourish on so exposed a site, where many of those 10,000 new trees were planted as wind-breaks, themselves needing protection as they established. There is natural shelter, Mark Driver told me, looking out on the spectacular 180-degree view from the estate office window and pointing to a ridge that lies in the way of the prevailing south-westerly wind. Being so close to the sea, he added, has the advantage of reducing the risk of late frosts – which, if they do occur, tend to roll down to non-planted areas rather than damage the vines.

Time will tell whether the site is viable and how its sparkling wines, released from 2018, will be received. Driver is optimistic. England is now the best place in the world to grow sparkling wine grapes, he says, with the current climate much more favourable than that of the Champagne region. A longer, slower ripening time brings full phenolic ripeness, with good fruit flavours and the right balance of sugar and acidity. English sparkling wine is right not only for the domestic market but also for worldwide sale. 'The UK is a massive importer of wine, a massive market for sparkling wine. It is not a question of why should we produce sparkling wine, but why not. English sparkling wine is the best sparkling wine in the world and its quality will continue to rise. Being part of it is exciting.'

A Frenchwoman's English enthusiasm

While Rathfinny attracts much public attention, Exton Park Vineyard has a quieter profile. But, from its first releases in 2015 it has proved, under the very assured control of head winemaker Corinne Seely, that great sparkling wines can be made on southern England's chalk hills. The vines grow, again high, south-east of Winchester on land that local watercress and super-market salad magnate Malcolm Isaac bought in 2009. The three champagne classics had been planted there over the previous six years and initially all the grapes were sold to the nearby Coates & Seely estate. But in

Corinne Seely delights in the chalk of Exton Park – here excavated from the new cellar. AUTHOR

2011 Isaac decided it was time to create Exton Park's own wines. Which was when Seely was drawn in, offered a blank drawing board and a very generous budget to create exactly the winery she wanted if she would accept the post of head winemaker. How could she refuse?

Although the site is high and open, it is further inland than Rathfinny. Seely has no problem with the exposure – though her assertion when we walked the vineyard early in 2017 that 'there's no frost' was over-optimistic, as the lowest-lying area suffered on those exceptional nights that followed in April – and she is ecstatic about the geology. 'I'm amazed by the soil. There is more chalk here than in Champagne.'

Never before, in a flying winemaking career that has taken her from Bordeaux to the Douro, from Australia to Languedoc, has Corinne Seely worked so closely with a vineyard manager. Fred Langdale, who studied at Plumpton after a stint in New Zealand's Central Otago region, and whose previous English experience was at Davenport and Nyetimber, describes Exton Park as 'a viticulturist's dream'. Both he and Seely revel in the diversity of the 22-hectare vineyard itself and the different rootstocks, different vine clones, different density of planting there. For Seely, who ferments each variety and every plot separately in her galaxy of small tanks, that is reflected in the

A winter morning at Exton Park – frost before the buds burst is no problem for the vines. EXTON PARK VINEYARD

Solar panels power the Exton Park winery. AUTHOR

ready-to-blend juice: for example, from the 2016 harvest she had a palette of twenty-three different potential components available for the delicious pinot noir-dominated Exton Park Brut. Her creed is: 'The winemaker's role is to interpret terroir, to be as neutral as possible to let that and the vines speak.'

From the moment of her appointment, a decision was taken that was unusual for England: only non-vintage sparkling wine would be produced. One-third of the harvest goes into reserve wines, to provide the 'library' that allows consistent wines to be achieved year on year, whatever the weather does. It is another example of the investment that Isaac has been happy to make, as is the solar-powered winery, with its two Bucher nitrogen-blanket presses. Grapes travel from vine to winery in five minutes, says Seely with little understatement, 'and it would be crazy to lose that freshness by oxygen contact during pressing'. Such protection is essential during the unusually long, slow pressing on which she stubbornly insists. Successfully avoiding any oxidation of the juice is one reason why she creates such delicately coloured and freshly flavoured wines.

There is no intention to extend the vineyard area (which should in the best years produce some 100,000 bottles), to use grapes from elsewhere or to undertake any contract winemaking. Nor will the estate become a wine tourism destination. For Seely, the future for Exton Park is simple: to be 'one of the best ambassa-dors of English wine'. She explained why: 'I believe in English terroir and I want to show people we are not just making a copy of champagne, we are making our own style of sparkling wine. I am very proud to be here at this beginning of the blossoming of the English wine industry. But we are not there yet. There is a long staircase to climb and we are in the middle of it now.'

New wine with old roots

Over the hills to the south-east, 7 kilometres from Exton Park, lies the vineyard where twentieth-century commercial viticulture was founded. How much has changed at Hambledon, sixty years on. Here, as at Exton Park, a huge hole has been dug into the chalk, to provide a new cellar with a constant 10-degree celsius temperature for the storage of maturing wines. Alongside it, a tasting room can immediately demonstrate the geology that owner Ian Kellett believes is so crucial: 'This is not just chalk, not just Champagne chalk, but the chalk of the very best part of Champagne, the Côte des Blancs.'

Hambledon is another to focus firmly on non-vintage wines, which are made under the direction of a winemaker from Champagne, Hervé Jestin – the biggest name on his CV is 6-million-bottle-a-year Duval-Leroy. In France now Jestin works on a much smaller scale, seeking the very best in champagnes, and he is happy to be involved in England as well. The freshness, acidity and fruit, he says, resemble what

Hambledon vines, not a cricket bat in sight. CHRIS DIXON PHOTOGRAPHY/AMBLEDON VINEYARD

was great in champagne thirty years ago. Kellett has total confidence in his ability: 'He is one of the world's best winemakers. He has made 250 million bottles of champagne!'

There is a further link with that particular French wine region at Hambledon. Looking out from the top of the winery, vines can be seen high on the skyline on Old Winchester Hill to the north. This is the Meonhill vineyard, planted in 2004 by champenois Didier Pierson. After a decade, Pierson returned home and, although he retained a consulting interest in the winemaking, the vineyard became part of the main Hambledon estate.

Chardonnay is the main focus of the modern plantings, flourishing as it never did in the days of Sir Guy Salisbury-Jones, and a variety of clones and rootstocks in all three noble varieties provide a broad blending choice for Jestin. Contract winemaking helps make best use of serious investment in equipment – crowd-funding and EU grants have contributed to the cost of that. But if the label says 'Hambledon', the wine will have come only from Hambledon-grown grapes. That reminds me of an issue Salisbury-Jones had over whether he should make sparkling wine. If he did, he told a questioner in the 1970s, he would need to bring in grapes from other vineyards and so couldn't put his vineyard's name on the bottles. No, he said, if it couldn't be called Hambledon, he didn't want to make it.

Like the unpressed grapes, I journeyed up three levels in the winery lift to where the two Coquard presses sit, with space for a third alongside. From pressing onwards, all transfer through the winery is by gravity, to ensure the gentlest handling of the wine-to-be. The scale is big – there is capacity to make 1.1 million bottles a year. Sales supremo Steve Lowrie anticipates there will be a ready market for them all. 'We're two-and-a-half to three years ahead of where we expected demand would be,' he told me as construction began on the new cellar in spring 2017. 'We can sell all we produce. Five years ago we were begging sommeliers and trade buyers to come and taste. Now they are asking us.'

Fermentation tanks in the Hambledon winery.
HAMBLEDON VINEYARD

Ian Kellett has brought a unique combination of previous skills to the estate he has owned since 1999 (and he also brought in his builder brother Philip, to take charge of the hole-digging). His academic background is in biochemistry, his high-flying City career was in global equity research focused on the food and drink sectors, and he has studied winemaking at Plumpton College. The path he is on now is far from low cost – around £10 million has been spent – but he promises that his past experience and contacts have given him access to the further funds that will be necessary to achieve Hambledon's ambitions. Much more rewarding, he argues, is to build a big business from a small base than to start with a fortune. 'I want to take England's earliest vineyard and develop the brand to the size of Pol Roger – one million bottles a year,' he said when Hampshire's vineyards held a group tasting in spring 2017. 'There is decent English sparkling wine and there is spectacular English sparkling wine. We are aiming to make the best English sparkling wine bar none, to become the standard bearer for English sparkling wine.'

Another county . . .

So far, all these sparkling wine estates have been located in Hampshire or Sussex. The UK county with the largest vineyard area, however, is Kent, and it is here that further ambitious plantings of the three champagne varieties have been taking place. The first by a major champagne house in England understandably caused something of a media storm. But, close to Taittinger's much-publicized vines at Chilham, others are growing, with much less hype.

Ruth and Charles Simpson made their decision to become vignerons – the French term is deliberate, for reasons that will soon become clear – in the most unusual of locations, Azerbaijan. Newly married, their careers had taken them both to that troubled place. We must, they decided, do something different. An idea began to grow. Wine was a shared pleasure and, although they had no viticultural or winemaking background, the thought of creating their own, of controlling the whole process from vine to bottle, appealed. They were to prove quick learners. Initial plans were to head to Australia, but what actually happened, says Charles Simpson, was 'a new world project in an old world area'. 'It was never our intention to end up with what we have got – an amazing sixteenth-century château. It was way more than we could afford, a recurring theme of our lives.' The many UK consumers of wines from Domaine Sainte Rose in the Languedoc surely delight in the fact that the couple didn't take the advice of their consultant, James Herrick, to 'sit down in a dark room until the thought had gone away'.

Why, though, leave southern France's sunshine for cooler, damper Kent? First, as they made clear to me, they haven't abandoned the Languedoc. Domaine

Château Sainte Rose, where the Simpson family's wine story began.
SIMPSONS WINE ESTATE

Sainte Rose had reached optimum size and there were no plans to expand. They are happy to leave its day-to-day running in the hands of the competent team there; the commercial side, where the Simpsons' expertise is much harder to replace, can be handled from England and on regular trips back. Second, it was time to make a decision about their daughters' secondary education, and England was the choice. And third, English wine had become a serious proposition. Serious enough then – 2012 – for an estate agent to be advertising a site in Kent as ideal for viticulture. That meant a premium price had been put on the land, much more than regular agricultural use would have justified. As part of the bargaining process, the would-be buyers pointed out that such optimistic promotion was all very well, but until vines were planted and thriving, there was no guarantee of the site's suitability. They recognized, though, the potential for making fine-quality sparkling wine there. 'It was the ideal project and a very exciting one,' Ruth Simpson told me. The two blocks that most tempted them were 'in our minds the perfect spot' – south-facing, good slopes, chalk 30 centimetres below the topsoil, old woodland around for protection, in an area with some of the highest sunshine hours in the UK. They ended up buying 30 hectares rather than the 10 they had intended.

It was, they say, the Languedoc all over again – buying into a wine area where land was undervalued compared with the likes of Bordeaux or Burgundy and therefore more affordable. 'It's very much the same spirit – get in early, be part of shaping and establishing an area.'

But this time around they have the experience to be independent, to avoid following exactly the same route as many other new English sparkling wine producers. Not for them the same vine suppliers and planting teams, nor necessarily the same vineyard and winery equipment. The nurseryman they knew from Sainte Rose brought 40,000 vines to Kent in a white Transit van, 'and we made huge savings'. Their

The French do it . . . vine planting on Simpsons English estate.
SIMPSONS WINE ESTATE

Young vines on Gusbourne's Kent estate. GUSBOURNE

experience has taught them where they do need to invest. For example, a nitrogen-blanket Bucher press is important to protect newly picked grapes from too much oxygen contact. And they have experience of producing bottle-fermented sparkling wine, which they have been able show to potential buyers long before release of their first English wines. Still wines – a blanc de noir pinot and a chardonnay – sit alongside the fizz, but the Simpsons' English focus is very strongly on sparkling wine, with a broad choice of clones and rootstocks to give a diversity of flavours in the base wines and complexity in the finished result.

But, as was the case in France, the new business will stretch them. 'Viticulture so much further north is an incredible challenge, in terms of winemaking, in what we are doing and most importantly knowing where we are going to sell the wine,' says Charles Simpson. That last issue has been sorted, initially at least. Within six months of the 2016 grapes being picked, more than

half of the 22,000 bottles from the vintage had been sold, and paid for, two years before their release.

And the English weather has smiled on them. Their first two harvests, in 2015 and 2016, were excellent, so much so in 2016 that photos of the grape pickers posted on Facebook convinced many followers that the location was the Languedoc, not Kent. An encouraging initial stock of wine has been cellared, but they are reckoning on facing two catastrophic years every decade. Such anticipation comes, again, from experience: 'We did learn from the school of hard knocks – second time around we know what we are doing.'

Two sites, for security and variety

Among England's most ambitious sparkling wine producers, there are some who prefer not to keep all their eggs in a single county basket. Gusbourne splits its vineyards between Kent (its first and larger site, 60 hectares) and West Sussex, half that area. There are obvious differences in soil: on the Kent site it is heavier, clay and sand, slower to warm in spring but holding its heat well to speed up autumn ripening; the Sussex vines are on flint and chalk.

In Kent, the vines grow on the Saxon shoreline, an escarpment just above the present coastal plain, with plots varying from 5 to 45 metres above sea level. The site is 10 kilometres from the coast – Dungeness power station is on the horizon – and the sea breeze reduces disease risk by wafting away mildew spores that would settle in more stagnant air. Winemaker and company CEO Charlie Holland describes the growing principles as 'responsibility, sustainability'. Herbicides are being phased out, though fungicides remain essential; grass or cover crops are grown between rows to avoid soil compaction. Roses, traditionally planted in vineyards as an early warning of disease rather than for decoration, grow at the end of each row here. They are red when the vines are pinot noir, pink for pinot meunier and white for chardonnay.

Despite this very modern use of the land, there is, says Holland, 'an enormous sense of history'. The estate dates back to 1410 and the three-geese crest of its then owner, John de Gusbourne, is revived in the label of the wines. A bomb crater remains from the Second World War, and Civil War musket balls are turned up by vineyard tractors, as was a 4,000-year-old flint scraper that could have been used by prehistoric fishermen to skin their catch. 'People have been working this land for thousands of years. It makes you feel very insignificant,' says their twenty-first-century successor.

Back in the present, Gusbourne wines are highly regarded, with justification. Charlie Holland's approach is straightforward: 'There are no real secrets, only time and patience.' Having the two separate vineyard areas is valuable, and not just for the differences between the fruit from each. Harvests can vary between the two, sometimes one compensating for a bad year at the other. No grapes are bought in, or sold. Pressings of fruit from the fourteen individual plots and from the forty different clones are kept apart as much as possible, to provide a huge choice of components for the sparkling

wine blending process. 'Some blends present themselves immediately, others take six weeks to create,' Holland told me. Fine still pinot noir and chardonnay are made, too, but they are secondary to the fizz.

With the most of the vineyard plantings in or near to full production, the latest investment has been in creating a new visitor centre, 'a proper experience, not just a shop'. 'We want to show people what we have.' And with London an hour away there is a big potential audience for one-off events as well as regular tours and tastings. What is poured into visitors' glasses will normally be finished wines, but I was privileged to be led through a selection of 2016 tank samples, before the base wine had undergone second fermentation. In Champagne, the experience would have been pretty hard going; here there was an enjoyable fruit character alongside the necessary acidity. I would have finished off, most happily, a glass rather than a sample of the blanc de blancs base. It had the salty tang that Holland seeks in that particular wine. 'I'm looking for minerality, an almost saline flavour,' he explained. 'Certain sites here have that salty character, a terroir effect.'

All Gusbourne sparkling wines are vintage, and Holland was particularly happy with the juice from the 2016 grapes, which gave a huge variety of flavours, needed virtually no sugar addition to achieve the desired final alcohol level and was high in acid. 'I like to reflect every year, to show our difference, the slightly different interpretations.' But reaching the heights he is aiming for needs very considerable amounts of that essential

Charlie Holland: 'There is a terroir effect.' GUSBOURNE

patience: 'Getting to know your vines is a ten-year process; getting to know your wine is also a ten-year process.' Given what had been achieved before the end of the first decade, the future should be exceptional.

Go west, to complete a career

Time now to journey from east to west, to another county where there is chalk and fine fizz. Looking out over the bowl of land that is the Spurrier family's Bride Valley Vineyard, near Bridport in Dorset, it is easy to understand why sheep have largely – though not entirely – made way for vines. The view is spectacular, the slopes inviting, the topsoil soon gives way to the western English edge of the chalk that stretches across to Champagne's vineyards. This, says the estate website, is 'where the English countryside sparkles'.

One wonders, perhaps, why Steven Spurrier waited so long before persuading his wife Bella that

Steven and Bella Spurrier. BRIDE VALLEY VINEYARD

the main crop from her farm should be wine rather than lamb and wool. As everyone with any professional or serious amateur interest in wine knows, the man behind the Judgement of Paris immersed himself in communicating about wine – as a critic, writer, teacher, consultant, retailer – from that French revolutionary

Bride Valley, where vines have replaced sheep. BRENDAN BUESNEL/BRIDE VALLEY VINEYARD

time onwards. 'The unsung hero of the wine world', 'inspirational', 'without doubt one of the most influential wine professionals of our time', 'a joy to go tasting with', 'always ahead of the curve': these and many more tributes flowed when he was made *Decanter* magazine's Man of the Year in 2017. Only in 2008, as he celebrated five decades in wine, did Spurrier decide it was time to create his own and join the English sparkling wine revolution.

The Bride Valley site is high, with vineyards running up from 75 metres to almost 170. Two large blocks of chardonnay, pinot noir and pinot meunier were planted in 2009, with later additions, of chardonnay in particular, to reach the present 10 hectares. The approach by vineyard manager Graham Fisher is pragmatic, 'sustainable rather than organic' farming. Herbicides were on the way out when I visited in spring 2017 and wildflowers were in, to encourage the right environment for natural predators. 'With somewhere like this you don't want to screw it up by spraying vast quantities of chemicals,' says Fisher. So some sheep have stayed, as 'organic lawnmowers'.

The wine is made by Ian Edwards at his Furleigh Estate, 15 kilometres away on the other side of Bridport. He believes in minimal intervention, and the resulting Brut Reserve NV is delicate and complex, while the vintage Bella Rosé has added fruit intensity. In both, there is a higher proportion of pinot meunier than many growers choose. It helps to define the wines' character. Champagne makers have told Bella Spurrier that they can detect a similarity to wines they knew from the 1970s, but they are no longer planting the grape as rising temperatures have robbed it of acidity. That is certainly not a problem at Bride Valley, where it is difficult to ripen pinot meunier fully on all but the most favourable slopes.

Despite the challenges posed by a place exposed more than many to the rigours of the English climate, there is a happy community feel to the Bride Valley estate. The family involvement stretches down a generation – the Spurriers' daughter Kate is in charge of marketing – and local people help with the harvest, although the estate isn't open to visitors. Small is beautiful seems an apt summing up, all the more so as the Bride happens to be southern England's shortest river, a mere 11 kilometres from its source to the English Channel.

The farmer's daughter comes home

The Spurriers decided not to invest in their own winery, hence the involvement of Furleigh Estate. This is the vineyard and winery project of two actuaries, Rebecca and Ian Edwards, with a shared passion for wine. Their main site, tucked away deep in the Dorset countryside, chose itself. The former dairy farm was where Rebecca Edwards grew up, though meanwhile her father had sold it. He had never imagined it as a vineyard, but he lived long enough after the couple bought it – they exchanged contracts on Christmas Eve 2004 – to see the new venture take off. With a second vineyard near Charmouth, the Edwards have just over 7 hectares planted, with germanic varieties

Promise for the future: the next generation of Edwards will benefit from their parents' investment. AUTHOR

for still wines alongside the champagne classics. It is a small but smart operation, with Ian Edwards – who studied at Plumpton once he had taken the decision to change career – in charge in the winery, and Rebecca handling administration.

Recognition came fast, with the first vintage, 2009, of the Classic Cuvée carrying off a gold medal in the 2012 Effervescents du Monde competition. It was the first English wine to do so, and one of only 38 gold-medal winners among more than 500 sparkling wines lined up before the judges. That wine also won the English wine trophy at the 2013 International Wine Challenge. The medal haul has continued, and is one of the enticements for visitors to brave the narrow lanes to visit Furleigh, to tour the vineyard, glass in hand, and try more wines in the attractive tasting room. How many visitors manage to spot, in the winery, the names of the Edwards' children embossed on three of the fermentation tanks? They are there, the guide suggests, as a promise of compensation to come after

their parents spent the next generation's heritage on the best winery equipment.

Let's find some more to taste

There are so many more excellent sparkling wine producers, but too little space to profile them in detail. Here, though, are a few tasters.

Coates & Seely, near Whitchurch, in Hampshire's Test Valley, has some very prestigious French connections: co-owner Christian Seely is the head of AXA Millésimes, charged with running top wine estates in Bordeaux, Languedoc, the Douro Valley and Hungary (though none in Champagne). The English estate, developed from a germ of an idea in 2006 by Seely and his ex-City-financier friend Nicholas Coates, is establishing its own prestige status in the UK, carrying off the supreme champion trophy in the inaugural UK Wine Awards in 2017. The wine so lauded was La Perfide 2009 blanc de blancs, one of the first wines made at

The Coates & Seely Wooldings vineyard. DANIEL DYTRYCH/COATES & SEELY

Coates & Seely. Besides awarding it the champion title, the judges named La Perfide best overall sparkling wine and best sparkling blanc de blancs. They also rewarded its pink twin sister with the best sparkling rosé trophy.

The partners do enjoy gentle digs at the French. The rather obvious 'perfidious Albion' implication is matched by their use of the term 'méthode britannique' to describe how their wines are made. They have also tried, without too much success, to introduce 'britagne' as the generic name for classic-blend sparkling wines from the northern shores of the English Channel.

It took more than a year from the initial business plan to finding the right vineyard. Wooldings lies in a steep, sheltered valley on the north Hampshire downs, where heat-retaining flints litter the soil and chalk is never far from the surface. Conveniently, Nicholas Coates lives close by. Part of the land had already been planted with champagne-variety vines, and in 2008 more went in. But the 12 hectares aren't enough to feed the state-of-the-art winery, so typically 25–30 per cent of the grapes are bought in from other Hampshire chalk-based vineyards.

Recognition of the wines, the UK supreme champion award in particular, has delighted both partners. Seely regards it as strong confirmation of the reasoning behind the estate, a belief 'that it might be possible to make sparkling wines here in England, from specific sites, in our case Hampshire chalk, that would be expressions of something uniquely English and that could one day be ranked among the best sparkling wines in the world'. It is, he adds, a 'miracle' that such high quality has been achieved in so short a time.

Domaine Evremond, Chilham, Kent, is coming into that ranking contest with a very relevant heritage – its vineyard is the first in England created by a champagne house. With a great media flourish, Pierre-Emmanuel Taittinger, president of Champagne Taittinger, his wife Claire and daughter Vitalie dug into the chalky soil of a former apple orchard not far from Canterbury on a damp May morning in 2017 and planted the first of the pinot noir, pinot meunier and chardonnay vines on the 40-hectare site. They are destined to provide, once in full production, some 300,000 bottles a year,

Domaine Evremond planting: Pierre-Emmanuel Taittinger (right) with Patrick McGrath, managing director of Hatch Mansfield, and Stephen Skelton watching on the sidelines. THOMAS ALEXANDER PHOTOGRAPHY/DOMAINE EVREMOND

the first release scheduled for 2023. The site is not as high as some, at around 80 metres, but windbreaks are still needed and Italian alder trees, the choice for many vineyards, went in ahead of the vines.

The estate's name commemorates the seventeenth-century importer of pre-fizz wine from the Champagne region, Charles de Marguetel de Saint Denis de Saint-Evremond, who we met earlier in this chapter, and the initiative is a joint venture with UK wine agency Hatch Mansfield, which imports Taittinger champagne. Appropriately, Hatch Mansfield has a long involvement with English wine – it introduced Castell Coch's wines to Londoners in the 1890s. Friends of both companies are backing it, too. The aim, says Pierre-Emmanuel Taittinger, is 'to create something special to show our appreciation of the UK support for Champagne'.

Mannings Heath, close to Horsham, West Sussex, is another of the new breed of high-input commercial investments, and its first vines were planted just a week earlier than Domaine Evremond's. With more added in spring 2018, the total vineyard area is 14 hectares. The sparkling wine culture is very serious, under the direction of Johann Fourie, former chief winemaker at South African giant KWV, but the vineyard isn't a stand-alone project. It is part of a South African concept, a golf and wine estate. Why all this South

African emphasis? Mannings Heath, already an established golf club, was bought in 2016 by Penny Streeter, an astute businesswoman, born in Africa and owner since 2013 of Benguela Cove vineyard and its associated restaurants and hotel in the Cape wine region. The less popular of the two courses at her new Sussex enterprise was halved in size, and the classic champagne varieties have replaced golfers on what were the fairways and greens of the discarded nine holes.

Viticulturist Duncan McNeil believes the sheltered site and deep silty, sandy loam over a sandstone subsoil should encourage great fruit flavours in the grapes. Even more crucial than soil, he argues, is climate – and those sheltering trees protect the Mannings Heath vines from the prevailing winds. 'The heat generated here won't be blown away.' Frost protection would not be necessary, he told a questioning journalist at the vineyard press launch. 'The best way to prevent frost damage is: don't plant vines in a frost-prone site.'

Johann Fourie also makes the Benguela Cove wines – he was happy to seize the opportunity to move from a huge operation to somewhere much smaller and more specific. He splits his time between the two hemispheres, but is increasingly at Mannings Heath as the vines crop in wine-realistic quantity. The chance to be in at the beginning of a new venture, to take his passion for sparkling wine further and to work in a cool-climate region 'ticked all the boxes – how could I say no?'.

Johann Fourie, Penny Streeter and Duncan McNeil as the first vines are planted at Mannings Heath. AUTHOR

He is looking to make chardonnay-dominated wines, with elegance and finesse. The first should be available in 2023.

Wiston Estate, Washington, West Sussex, has a South African connection, too, in the person of Pip Goring. The gestation period for her vineyard, however, was far longer than for Streeter's. The land has belonged to the Goring family since 1743, used to grow crops and raise beef cattle and sheep. When Pip married owner Harry, she brought an interest in wine from her home in Cape Town – her French Huguenot ancestors had established a vineyard in Franschoek. But it took thirty-four years to convince her husband to convert 6.5 of Wiston's 243 hectares to vines. Chardonnay, pinot noir and pinot meunier went into the chalk-based soil in 2006. Dermot Sugrue – who had just left Nyetimber – came on board as winemaker, and a winery was created in a disused turkey factory, its two levels allowing the pressed juice to move by gravity from the upper to the lower for the rest of the minimally intrusive processing.

The intention, right from scratch, was to make 'terroir wines', Sugrue declared to the crowds round the Wiston table at one of 2017's major bubbly trade shows in London. 'Eleven years down the line we feel vindicated. The wines are a true expression of sense of place.' While he recognizes, in a very similar way to Cherie Spriggs, the differences between grapes grown on chalk or on greensand, he was not yet ready in 2017 to accept the argument that grapes from Sussex and Hampshire chalk have separate identities. Differing winemaking styles have more effect than county boundaries, he argued.

Charles Palmer Vineyards, close to the sea at Winchelsea in East Sussex, is another of England's family farms where the crop has changed. Its eponymous owner was born in New Zealand, came to his family's home county as an eight-year-old and followed his parents into conventional agriculture. In 2006 he planted his first 2 hectares of vines and is moving towards ten times that, anticipating a 50,000-bottle production when the wines from 2019 – his tenth vintage – are ready for sale. The classic trio of varieties, all for sparkling wine, have their roots in soil more burgundian than champenois and are planted at low density, to give room for disease-preventing air movement and to encourage fewer but riper grapes than would be found on more crowded vines. Investment is carefully measured, but Palmer is well aware that scaling up is potentially the profitable route – the vineyard 'has to stand on its own feet'. Importantly for that, the wines are very good indeed.

Hattingley Valley, near Alresford, Hampshire, is the achievement of a long-term dream by owner Simon Robinson, lawyer by profession. It's a big set-up, with 24 hectares of vineyards on two sites plus plenty of contract winemaking work. And it made big news in May 2016 when a link-up with Pommery was announced, with Thierry Gasco, chef de cave at the champagne house, working with Hattingley Valley head winemaker Emma Rice on a cuvée carrying the Pommery name. Wines from Pommery's own English vines are likely to follow. Just before that announcement, but rather less widely publicized, was the introduction of the first apprenticeship scheme in the UK wine industry, in which Robinson's company is in partnership with the Worshipful Company of Vintners. First recruit on the two-year full-time scheme, which blends practical work in the winery with study at Plumpton College, was Zoë

Inside the Hattingley Valley winery, with Coquard press and oak barrels. HATTINGLEY VALLEY

Driver. Seven months after she started at Hattingley Valley, and to coincide with National Apprenticeship Week 2017, the former travel industry worker gave an enthusiastic interview. Despite the 'hard, frustrating, laborious' work, she was relishing the opportunity. 'As clichéd as it sounds, I actually look forward to going to work every morning – I love what I do.' Her ambition is one day to make her own wine.

Hattingley Valley's core wines are from the champagne varieties, characterized by discreet inclusion of wine fermented in old burgundy barrels. There has, as well, been an experiment with bottle-fermenting a blend of bacchus and pinot gris; the result is an attractive, fruit-led wine that hints at the potential for good English fizz at slightly lower prices – a challenge to crémant rather than to champagne.

Hattingley Valley's James Matyear lays out boxes ready for the harvest at Cottonworth Vineyard.
THE ELECTRIC EYE PHOTOGRAPHY/ HATTINGLEY VALLEY

Fox & Fox, with vineyards around Mayfield in East Sussex, regularly makes a sparkler from pinot gris with just a touch of chardonnay. Pinot gris is much underrated, says co-owner Jonica Fox, arguing that the long English ripening season allows its grapes to develop great aromatics and depth of flavour. There is a mosaic of soils in the two vineyards, which together total 10 hectares: sands, silts and clays overlying sandstone and shale. 'Mosaic', appropriately, is the name of the classic-blend cuvée.

Greyfriars, on the Hog's Back in Surrey, bottle-ferments a noble but non-champagne variety, sauvignon blanc. Interesting as that is, it is incidental to the main emphasis on more classic styles of sparkling wine from the champagne grapes – the oaked blanc de blancs and rosé brut are garlanded with silver medals. Mike and Hilary Wagstaff bought a small existing vineyard, already concentrating on champagne varieties, in 2010. They have added a further 15 hectares of vines, intend to plant more and are expanding the on-site winery to handle an anticipated 100,000-bottles-a-year production.

Bluebell Vineyard Estates, in Ashdown Forest in East Sussex, is hardly little Switzerland, despite the slopes of its 25 hectares of vineyards around the winery and further afield in Sussex. Yet it is experimenting with a grape popular below the Alps but hardly seen in England other than in private gardens. Chasselas, winemaker Kevin Sutherland believes, could be turned into decent entry-level sparkling wine or, in very good years, a still dry white. Time will tell, but the grape-handling skill is there. Sutherland's lengthy commitment to English wine shows in the very fine classic wines he makes. Notable among these is a late-disgorged blanc de blancs 2008, an impressive example of the richness and depth Sussex-grown chardonnay fizz can acquire if given years resting on its lees in a calm cellar. He makes a very enjoyable traditional-method seyval blanc too.

Something else ensures Bluebell is memorable: the slogan that reflects the previous use of the vineyard land around the present winery. The late twentieth-century occupants were pigs, some 10,000 of them. Inevitably, the 'swine into wine' moniker has stuck.

Hush Heath Estate, Staplehurst, Kent, where vines grow in deep Wealden clay soils, also has an unusual emphasis to its wine. But unlike those estates introducing bubbles in non-champagne-variety wines, its point of reference is colour. Rosé has been Hush Heath's calling card since the first vintage of Balfour Brut in 2004,

Never a pig in sight: Bluebell's land is now for vine, not swine.
BLUEBELL VINEYARD ESTATES

which carried off a gold medal and trophy at the 2008 International Wine Challenge. Now, alongside the continuing vintage rosé releases, there is a non-vintage dry rosé, classic-method white and red fizz, plus rosé, white and red still wines. Next to the vines, extended to cover 20 hectares, are apple orchards, and winemakers Owen Elias and Victoria Ash create smart 8 per cent alcohol sparklers from cox, egremont russet and bramley juice – one of those is pink, too.

At Hush Heath, as at Nyetimber, there is a timbered Tudor manor house, built in 1503 as home for two families of wealthy weavers. That date is commemorated in the label, Balfour 1503, of the non-vintage wines introduced in 2015. Owner Richard Balfour-Lynn acknowledges that vines were initially a hobby. They are very much more than that now.

Cottonworth, in Hampshire's Test Valley, is the English expression of owner Hugh Liddell's wider experience, although here the pinot noir and chardonnay varieties he first worked with making still wines in Burgundy are destined entirely for sparkling wine production. The farm has been in the Liddell family for four generations, but the wine initiative began only from 2005, after Hugh Liddell's return from a spell in Burgundy. With chalky soil and gentle slopes below 100 metres in height, it was a 'no brainer' to plant the three classic champagne varieties. His view of terroir is somewhat broader than that usually offered: he includes the history and traditions of the wine-growing region alongside the more conventional factors of soils, climate and human input. He acknowledges, however, that history and tradition are 'something we don't yet have in England'. Liddell is one of several of the new generation of wine producers who argue that England is very much a new-world wine country, despite its location on the edge of the old wine world. That new-world freedom from long-established rules has the advantage of allowing innovative thinking.

Cottonworth's grapes, from the 12 hectares of vines, soon became too much for the small on-site production facility, and winemaking moved to Hattingley Valley, 'a Titan of English wineries' in Liddell's description. He enjoys the character that Hattingley's practice of barrel fermentation for some base wine gives to the finished fizz.

Jenkyn Place Vineyard, on the eastern edge of the Hampshire chalk, between Alton and Farnham, was first and foremost chosen by Yorkshire-born property investor Simon Blagdon as a family home. What to do with the abandoned hop fields around the seventeenth-century house was a secondary consideration. But the hop poles were ugly and needed to go. Blagdon admits he had 'no desire to have a vineyard', until he tasted Nyetimber's wine. Those former hop fields were deemed ideal for vines, the first were planted in 2004 and by 2010 they covered the full 5 hectares available. As ever in England, there have been good years and bad. In 2011 and 2012, no wines were made under the Jenkyn Place label and the grapes were sold to others. Blagdon retains his Yorkshire frankness: 'The grapes were terrible, so I thought I would let someone else make bad wine with them.' Good years have seen the wines, made at Wiston by Dermot Sugrue, win many medals – including in China's biggest wine competition.

Court Garden, Ditchling, Sussex, is a very near neighbour to Ridgeview, and it was at the suggestion of Mike Roberts that the Corney family planted vines there in 2005, initially selling the fruit to Ridgeview. It was a good moment to diversify from sheep farming, which was still suffering the impact of the 2001 foot and mouth disease outbreak. (Sheep do remain on the farm, with a valuable role of tidying among the vines in winter.) Soon an on-site winery was built, with Plumpton-trained Hugo Corney – 'a refugee from the accountancy industry', says father Howard – making the wines. Two, both blanc de noirs from the 2010 vintage, make an interesting comparison. There was more base wine than was needed for the normal cuvée, so some of the spare spent time in oak barrels, to good effect.

All of Court Garden's wines come from on-site grapes, from vines growing in greensand-based soil. But to Howard Corney, the importance of soil is 'overstated – vines are very tolerant'. English weather has far more influence on results, he believes.

Harrow & Hope, Marlow, Berkshire, like so many of the new sparkling wine vineyards, is on chalk, but chalk

Where there were hops, now there are vines, at Jenkyn Place Vineyard. JENKYN PLACE VINEYARD

that presents a particular challenge. The vineyard site is an ancient Thames gravel terrace, the chalk overlain by clay soil thickly set with flint, which is 'a nightmare to work and cultivate'. So much so that the trials of creating the vineyard are remembered now in the name, inspired by broken harrows and the hope for the future of this small family enterprise.

Wine is in the blood. Henry Laithwaite, who has set up the business with his wife Kaye, is son of Tony Laithwaite, the man behind 700,000-customer Laithwaite's Wine, whose involvement with wine began five decades ago. Back from making wine in Bordeaux, because they wanted to raise a family in England, the couple were happy to start their 6.5-hectare venture in the Thames Valley – the slopes are ideal and there are high summer temperatures, though the frost threat remains (their vines suffered in 2016 and 2017). First

harvest was in 2013, and the wines have joined the medal-winning list. They are hoping for even better results in the future: it will, they accept, take time to appreciate fully the subtleties of the site. Land along the river from Marlow to Henley might become as desirable to future vine-growers as the Côte d'Or, Henry Laithwaite suggests, if only owners with no interest in wine would part with it.

He and Kaye pay tribute to many people in the industry who have helped them, notably the late Mike Roberts and Australian sparkling wine guru Tony Jordan, whose input into the winemaking on regular visits they value immensely. Around a third of the wine is fermented in well-used bordeaux barrels, which Henry Laithwaite argues gives a textural difference from stainless steel and is an advantage when grapes 'are not necessarily as ripe as you might like'. That, plus

malolactic conversion, means less sugar is needed at the dosage stage. Keeping a good stock of reserve wine is part of the long-term plan, and the brut reserve has been non-vintage from the beginning.

Westwell Wines, below the Pilgrims' Way on the North Downs in Kent (an appropriate location – remember Chaucer's heavily imbibing Canterbury-bound travellers), is an example of how smaller, lesser-known producers can shine in the most distinguished of company. Westwell, owned by John and Rids Rowe, carried off the International Wine Challenge 2017 English Sparkling Trophy for its 'layered and creamy' Special Cuvée 2014. There are 3.6 hectares of chardonnay and the two pinots, plus another 1.6 hectares of ortega for still wines. The vineyard may be small but the Rowes' ambition is big – to make the 'ultimate' English sparkling wine. John Rowe brings in his quality assurance experience at Proctor & Gamble to contribute towards that, and spreads his expertise to others in his new business. History plays a part, too. He has roots in wine – his mother comes from an Italian viticultural heritage stretching back generations.

Digby Fine English, Mayfair, London, with no vineyards at all, is rather different from all these, except that Dermot Sugrue, Wiston's winemaker, is part of the team. This is a 'négociant' operation: the company buys in grapes for its wine rather than growing its own. The idea came to founders Jason Humphries and Trevor Clough 'like a lightning bolt' as they visited a winery in Oregon. 'You should never follow a business dream that starts on holiday,' says Clough, but they did. Neither has a wine background, so, rather than join the planting horde, they decided on their different approach. They source the raw material, on long-term contracts, from vineyards through Kent, Sussex and Hampshire. From it they create two premium vintage wines, white and rosé, made only in the best years, and a white and rosé at a more introductory level.

Export, particularly to the USA, is crucial to the initiative's success, and Digby was the first English sparkling wine to win major retail distribution in Australia. Just before the announcement of their trophy win in the first UK Wine Awards, Clough set out their ambition: 'Our goal is to become the English luxury brand of fine wine. We have put a lot of effort into the lifestyle side of the business.' Paying for the right presentation as well as the right product is money well spent, he says. And the origin of the name of the company? Remember the Englishman who invented the bottle strong enough to allow wine to bubble away without shattering results.

Chapter 8

STILL IMPROVING: THERE IS MUCH MORE TO ENGLISH WINE THAN FIZZ ALONE

WHEN THE PIONEERS OF THE ENGLISH WINE revival first dug spades into soil they were planning almost without exception to make still table wines from the grape harvests to come. There had been early experiments with fizz – Raymond Barrington Brock had made a few bottles – but they were very much on the fringe of the main projects. So much has changed in fifty years.

But behind all the fuss over the fine sparkling wines that now go from English vineyards to a large number of the world's wine-drinking countries, a quantity of still wine continues to be produced. Good wines have been made for decades but, compared to much of what went before, the latest still wine has a much more mainstream appeal. Varieties proclaimed on bottle labels have largely moved on from the little-known reichensteiner or schönburger, for example. Instead, they are far more likely to be the star of the germanic grapes, bacchus, or such worldwide varieties as chardonnay and pinot blanc. I've deliberately referred to white grapes; red and rosé wines are produced in much lower quantities and, pinot noir excepted, they are most often blends of varieties whose names remain unfamiliar to most wine buyers.

The reasons for the quality improvements in still wines from UK vineyards are very much the same as those that have boosted the fizz: wise choice of vineyard location, matching of grape variety to site and choice of more appealingly flavoured varieties, better care of the vines, well-equipped and well-run wineries, enough money behind estates to see them survive the inevitable bad years, those rising growing-season temperatures and, vitally, the increased knowledge and profession-alism of growers and winemakers.

There's a third 'p' to be added to those of people and professionalism, and that is Plumpton. Plumpton Agricultural College, on the outskirts of a small Sussex village better known for its racecourse, has international repute in the wine world. It is the place that has, more than any other, boosted the quality of English wine of every kind. September 2018 is a date to celebrate – the thirtieth anniversary of the college wine department,

Plumpton student Stuart Graham and research bottles.
PLUMPTON COLLEGE

and for every one of those years it has been headed by the same man, Chris Foss.

As we sat in his small, cramped office (most of the wine centre building is devoted to generous spaces for teaching, research and winemaking), Chris Foss passed me a sheaf of information on the college wine courses. The final tightly typed A4 page listed graduates and the places to which they have moved to make wine or to work in marketing it. That list included almost every one of the best-known names in UK winemaking and almost every notable UK vineyard.

Plumpton College has its own vineyards, and makes (and regularly sells out of) sparkling wine as well as still. But the college's immeasurable value in helping to put English wine in the admirable position it holds today isn't defined by whether or not there are bubbles in the liquid. Wine in its many guises is what Plumpton teaches its students to make and market.

A Plumpton graduate, Simon Woodhead, is one of the most passionate makers of still wines I met as I researched this book. In the next chapter we will briefly tour his vineyard on Stopham Estate, set in a scenic Sussex valley; what is relevant here is some of the kit

and techniques he has developed to make still wines of optimum quality. Before changing career track, he was an engineer, designing sensors for McLaren Formula One cars. 'I like measuring things,' he confesses. And that led him to develop a computerized system to measure the amount of carbon dioxide – a natural product of grape-juice fermentation – given off in the tanks at the Stopham Vineyard winery. Things don't stop there. To help preserve the aromas in his wines, Woodhead wants a slow, steady, gentle fermentation, normally extending for six weeks. So his computer system uses the carbon dioxide emission information to adjust the temperature of the fermenting juice, by controlling the coolant between the double skins of his stainless steel tanks.

This automated measurement/temperature adjustment system is a very neat way of combining modern technology with the ancient technique of making wine, yet surprisingly it is seen in few other wineries. It shows how a newcomer, with a useful engineering background, can offer something innovative and valuable in an agricultural industry where tradition laid down over generations is so often revered.

Simon Woodhead: passionate about quality, from vine to bottle. AUTHOR

An array of small tanks, like these at Redbank winery, are part of the good winemaker's tools. DUNCAN LOUGHREY/SIXTEEN RIDGES

Gases to avoid, and poor weather to counteract

Whether their product is still wine or sparkling, winemakers must take care that their fermenting juice avoids one of the major wine dangers – too much oxygen. A little is needed during the primary phases of fermentation to avoid the production of hydrogen sulphide, which gives a rotten egg smell to the liquid, but too much oxygen contact causes wines to lose their freshness and fruitiness. To prevent that, Woodhead, like many meticulous winemakers, has sourced tanks of a variety of sizes, so juice from a small plot of grapes goes into a small tank and that from a larger plot goes into a larger one, minimizing exposure to oxygen. Additionally, some of the tanks are fitted with lids that slide down to sit on top of the juice and are then held in place by a kind of pumped-up 'tyre' around the edge, keeping the damaging gas at bay.

Too much carbon dioxide is a further wine production danger, but one that affects humans rather than the liquid. In extreme circumstances, the huge quantities that are produced during fermentation have caused the death of cellar workers, though not in the UK. In most wineries, danger levels diminish rapidly through natural or artificial ventilation and often alarms are fitted, but winemakers are not entirely joking should they warn visitors not to bend down to tie their shoelaces (carbon dioxide is heavier than air and builds up from ground level).

But the greatest challenge faced by English winemakers is the weather, especially rain at flowering (coinciding usually with Wimbledon fortnight) and cool temperatures at autumn ripening time. And for those concentrating on still wines, this makes life particularly difficult. Apart from reducing grape yields, poor weather leads to low sugars and high acidity and too little alcohol in the final wine. Freshness is a great characteristic of English wines, but no drinker wants

Vine coming into flower at Ridgeview Estate: rain at this stage will threaten yield and sugar levels. RIDGEVIEW ESTATE

to swallow a liquid so acidic that his or her teeth start to ache after only a single glass. Therefore intervention is necessary. Winemakers who go down the still route usually need to achieve an alcohol level of around 11.5 per cent if their wines are to be balanced and pleasant to drink. There are some English wines with much lower alcohol levels, but most of these must wait several years after bottling before their acidity softens, and they rarely match the quality of wines of more conventional strength. In all but the ripest years, chaptalization is needed to bring still wines to the preferred alcohol level, and that explains the big brown Tate & Lyle sacks seen in almost every UK winery. To raise the alcohol level by as little as 1 per cent a lot of sugar is needed: 100 kilos for a 3,000-litre tank of juice.

Of the various ways to reduce the acidity of grape juice during the winemaking process the most common is malolactic conversion. At Stopham, the method is different, though not unique – some other winemakers, including those at some champagne houses for example, also favour it. A chalk-based compound rather than a bacterium is the agent used to neutralize acid, and it does have a very English wine ring about it, even though Stopham's vines grow on sand rather than on the white rock. A small proportion of the juice in a tank is taken off and added slowly to the compound. Lots of whisking for good mixing is involved. Then the mix goes back into the tank and the result is the removal of equal amounts of both tartaric and malic acid.

This is done before fermentation begins, for Woodhead is adamant, as are many more of the UK's best winemakers, that minimum intervention afterwards leads to better wines. His wines are a splendid illustration of skill and science combined.

'Orange': an alternative to white, red and rosé

If this makes winemaking sound like a very industrial process, that is far from true at small, artisan wineries such as Stopham. International big-brand wine is often the result of much, much more interference, all through the production process. At the extreme other end of the

scale, however, it is highly risky to attempt to make wine simply by leaving grape juice to ferment naturally. The result all too often is vinegar. Even the most tenacious adherents of 'natural' wine need to exert some control over what happens, and while some of their results are fabulous, others can be very odd indeed.

But there is the beginning of something along those unconventional lines in England. The first English 'orange' wine was released by Chapel Down in autumn 2015, followed a year later by another from Litmus Wines, the wine consultancy and winemaking operation headed by John Worontschak and based at Denbies. For both wines, the bacchus grapes were fermented and aged on their skins in the same way as red wines are made, introducing tannins alongside acidity and giving very dry, nutty-edged flavours. This historic practice is becoming fashionable again in lots of winemaking countries and there are London restaurants with entire 'orange' sections in their lists. Most orange wines live up to their names, being appreciably deeper in colour than conventional white wines, but the English examples have deliberately been kept paler. Scent and flavour, though, are very different from the white wine norm: Worontschak himself described Litmus Orange as 'disorienting at first'. Taste on, however, and its character and complexities are intriguing.

Without going quite as far off piste as that, there is increasing interest among makers of still wine in using 'wild' yeasts, those that occur naturally on grape skins and stalks, instead of the manufactured ones created by chemists and sold in packets. Organic grower and winemaker Will Davenport is one who is faithful to natural yeasts, with results that are much respected by his peers. 'One grape variety, one yeast equals one-dimensional wine,' he argues. Instead, pick grapes at different times, with different levels of acidity, use not one but several natural yeasts, and the wine will have much more character.

The grape debate

The right choice of grape varieties to use for still wines remains an ongoing debate. There are plenty

Ripe pinot gris grapes growing at Stopham; the variety has potential in England. STOPHAM VINEYARD

of supporters of the long-grown germanic grapes, and plenty more who firmly favour names much more familiar from bottle labels worldwide. Probably the largest proportion of producers, though, reckon on a mix of the two as the best option in the UK.

Kevin Sutherland, whose long experience of English wine has already provided valuable input in Chapter 3's climate-change discussion, can contribute usefully here, too. He sees bacchus and ortega as the 'stand-out' varieties for still wine, with good potential from pinot blanc, pinot gris and chardonnay. And there will be more still wine, he believes. When we talked at the 2017 English Wine Producers' annual tasting, he was clear in his prediction: 'As peoples' understanding of winemaking increases and with the change in varieties I think we will see an equal split between still and sparkling, in the next ten to fifteen years.'

Mike Wagstaff at Surrey vineyard Greyfriars, one of the first to show that sauvignon blanc can now be successfully grown in England, urges others making still wine to choose internationally familiar grapes: 'If you can possibly grow them, get varieties that are well known.'

Bacchus is well on the way to fitting into that category. More and more wines are being made from a variety that enjoys life in England, and perhaps the least likely example hails from a former gin distillery in London SW8. London Cru (from late 2017 Roberson Wine) was set up in 2013 to make great wines from bought-in grapes, at the same time offering interested wine drinkers a chance to get involved in the process, alongside winemaker Gavin Monery. Joining in, said Monery, was a creative and innovative way to learn, 'in a fun way'. Initially, the grapes came from vineyards in Europe; from 2014, they were joined by homegrown product, from Kent and Essex. All London Cru wines are named after a landmark or street in the capital that has a phonetic link to the grape variety; 'Baker Street' is the choice for bacchus and, appropriately, the 2016

Bacchus grapes arrive at London Cru for processing. LONDON CRU vintage went on the list of one of Baker Street's best restaurants very soon after its launch.

Another grape variety is increasingly appearing in bottles of English still wine, though in an unusual form. Pinot noir is of course a classic component of fizz, and there are a good number of still red examples. Take the skins away from the juice quickly – as is done for white sparkling wine – and a 'white pinot' still wine is possible. The colour of the results varies: Albourne Estate's attractive, sophisticated offering is, to my eyes, closer to onion-skin rosé than white, but others can be hard to distinguish from white wines made from white grapes.

There is one category of wine that really can't have bubbles: ultimate sweet dessert wine. True, there are sweet sparkling wines that will pair with some puddings – Italian asti with Christmas pudding is one happy marriage – but fizz with the likes of apple pie, lemon cheesecake, summer pudding, mince pies? No. English dessert wine does, however, match well with all these sweet treats, helped by its acidity as well as its sweetness. It has a way to go to equal the world's finest high-acid stickies – think of Loire chenin blanc or Hungarian tokaji – but there are good examples from some of the germanic grapes, ortega particularly, though production quantities are tiny.

The essential factor in the creation of great sweet wine is that the grapes must lose most of their water content, usually by ripening far longer on the vine than those used for drier wines. For that, there must be a long, sunny autumn, not something the UK climate can guarantee. During the late-ripening period, if there is the right level of moisture in the air (from gently misty mornings, not day-long deluges), the fuzzy grey botrytis mould that can do such damage a little earlier is now welcome in the vineyard, becoming what is known as 'noble rot'. The juice pressed from these shrivelled, unappetising grapes has not only the sweetness of non-affected fruit but also a distinctive marmalade-y flavour.

There are other means of creating the concentrated juice needed for dessert wines – freezing the ripe grapes, for example, or drying them on straw mats in well-ventilated indoor spaces – but for now those remain principally German or Italian practices rather than English ones.

Chapter 9

A Tour Through More of the Vineyards

WINE IS A VERY INDIVIDUAL PLEASURE, AND the choice of vineyards profiled in this book is definitely my own, though I have tried to offer a selection of big and small, still and sparkling, conventional and organic, tourism-oriented or centred solely on wine. They are only a single-figure proportion of the total and many, many more will be of similar appeal to anyone wanting to understand English wine. If you've never tried it but are tempted, if you know a little but want to learn a lot, if you've had a less than enjoyable example years back but are wondering what the latest wines are like, go to all the vineyards you can, see the places, meet the people and taste the wines. That way it will all make much more sense, and once back home there will be few greater wine pleasures than picturing in your mind the vines whose fruit is in the glass in your hand.

This chapter is the result of my own explorations in 2017 (as were the sparkling wine producers' profiles in Chapter 7). There is every likelihood that the places I've visited and the people I've talked with will long remain important in the English wine industry, continuing to offer excellent wine and a welcoming experience to visitors. But if there have been changes by the time you read this book, I hope you will still enjoy the stories – and discover your own alternative experiences.

For all of the vineyards that welcome visitors, whether listed here or not, do your homework before turning up. Many may close for the winter or open only on particular days of the week; some will happily let visitors stroll through the vines unguided while others offer only advance-booked tours; most sell their own wines and may have on-site shops stocking other local produce; and some will run restaurants or cafés or even provide accommodation. Be aware that bad weather may force last-minute closures, and vineyard work – spraying or harvesting, for example – may restrict access.

Individual vineyard's websites should be the most up-to-date source of information, but for a broad overview of what's where and whether visitors are accepted, seek out the free *Vineyards Map of England and Wales* from WineGB or consult the *UK Vineyards Guide* by Stephen Skelton. Both are regularly updated. There are regional maps and wine trails, too, an interactive map on the WineGB website and one useful example of the increasing number of other good sources of online information is www.winecellardoor.co.uk.

Which way is best to order the virtual visits provided here? Regional or alphabetical would be the most obvious, but I'm going for themes: it makes sense to look at how the very biggest producers, for example, go about their business, or how those who follow the organic route compare, or why some make both sparkling and still wines while others stick with a single style. First of all, though, something else. In all the discussion about place and soil and weather and grape variety, about size or speciality, about bubbly or still, another crucial factor can too easily be forgotten. People make wine. Some – though I haven't met any in England – are insistently interventionist, manipulating their grapes and creating a product that bears little relation to what it is made of and where it comes from; others prefer to let nature take its course as much as they dare; and many more fall somewhere in between. But for me there is a category beyond any of these, where wine transcends the way in which it is actually made and where the final liquid reflects most of all the individual personality of the person who creates it.

So first off let's meet Peter Hall.

Breaky Bottom, near Newhaven, East Sussex: sparkling survivor, despite the odds

That reflection of personality, I'm convinced, is why Peter Hall's wines have consistently been loved by serious wine commentators, have received gold medal after gold medal after gold medal, and have been enjoyed at the highest tables in the land.

The place contributes, too. Breaky Bottom is snuggled deep into a hollow of the South Downs, in Hall's description, 'two hills from the sea'. There is, Oz Clarke has said, 'no more beautiful vineyard in Britain'. Hall is one of the institutions (in the best possible sense) of English wine. He planted his first vines in 1974 and, despite the area more than doubling since, they cover less than 2.5 hectares, equal to a mere 1 per cent of the land owned by his nearest wine neighbour, Rathfinny, 11 kilometres eastwards across the downs as the crow flies (or, more appropriately, the pheasant,

for reasons that will soon become clear). To quote Oz Clarke again: 'He has been felled by money, bureaucracy and nature, but has always struggled back to his feet and continued to make one of England's greatest sparkling wines.'

At Breaky Bottom, that often over-used designation microclimate is, for once, correctly applied. Exceptionally, the north-facing vineyard flowers and ripens first, while everything happens later at its rather more exposed south-facing partner. The breeze that is common to both reduces disease; the shape of the landscape shelters the vines from the prevailing south-westerly wind. 'Vines HATE wind' is Hall's mantra.

Such insistence on being right is surely why Breaky Bottom has survived as a vineyard well into its fifth decade, despite tribulations that would have forced any less stubborn a grower to quit. The floods came first, five of them, as heavy autumn rains poured off the bare arable fields above. The fifth, in 2000, was the worst. It severely damaged the vines and devastated the cottage with which Hall had fallen in love as a young worker on the farm and which he had slowly improved from a one-down, two-up, water-less, power-less near-hovel

Peter Hall, the survivor. AUTHOR

to a family home. He and his wife lived in a caravan for more than two years while the effects of the flood were resolved. After that came the pheasants, as a shooting estate replaced conventional farming on the land around the vineyard. With virtually no natural wooded habitat available, the birds descended on the vines, says Hall, and grapes destined for 30,000 bottles of wine were lost over successive seasons. More years of argument, litigation and insurance claims finally brought 'very small recompense'.

Throughout, wine continued to be made. Initially, Peter Hall had run the land as an animal-based smallholding, with pigs, sheep, calves and chickens. The suggestion of vines came when the owner of a vineyard on the Isle of Wight visited and remarked how suitable the site was for what then was a very new crop for twentieth-century English farmers. Easily available grape varieties were few, and the possibility of sparkling wine was never mentioned, so Hall settled for the germanic classics of the period, seyval blanc and müller-thurgau: 'seyval had the edge, though I did make some very good müller-thurgau.' The golden haul began, with an International Wine Challenge top medal for the 1990 seyval. He planted more of the variety, pulled up the müller-thurgau, and from 1996 decided to indulge his love of fizz by making traditional-method sparkling wine. More medals. From 2002 he added champagne variety vines, chardonnay principally, to the seyval and continued with sparkling wine alone, both pure seyval and classic blends. These too struck gold. He grins: 'By golly, it has worked.'

His success is, he says, not down to climate change: 'I'm a cautious and responsible global warming sceptic,' he stressed as a warm March sun shone on his vines. He concedes that there is now rather less 'BAW' – 'bloody awful weather' – than in the 1970s and 1980s, but

There is less 'bloody awful weather' affecting Breaky Bottom these days. AUTHOR

believes the successful shift in grape varieties has come about because growers understand their vines so much better and select clones more suitable for England's climate. At Breaky Bottom Hall grows cuttings from his existing vines, with the intention of avoiding disease in new rootstocks.

In an effort to indulge his love of fine, elegant white wines he did try experimental plantings of Loire classics back in the 1970s, but their acidity was overwhelming. Now, if he was starting again, he would most likely plant only the three noble champagne grapes, just as so many of the new boys on the block have done. And as the French should, too. 'If you are a canny head of a champagne house you should look at the UK. No other country in the world can get similar quality,' he told me, emphasizing also how very much cheaper vineyard land is in England than in Champagne. The exponential growth of English sparkling wine seen over the last decade 'isn't finished yet', he adds.

Hall is intensely close to his land, seeing himself as one individual in a history that stretches back 300,000 years – he has Acheulean hand axes found in the vineyard to prove it. 'I love this little valley.'

Camel Valley, near Wadebridge, Cornwall: sunny spot, smiling sippers

Visits to Breaky Bottom are necessarily by appointment: apart from factors such as Peter Hall's need, as an almost entirely one-man operation, to spend most of his time among the vines, access is by a poorly signed 2-kilometre track, heavily rutted and certainly no route for wine tourists looking for a smart day out. At Camel Valley, where personality – that of the Lindo family – is also paramount, things are rather different. Brown tourist-attraction signs lead visitors off the nearby Padstow to Bodmin main road, along a winding lane and up the hill into the vineyard and a generous car parking area. Close by are cycle racks for those two-wheeled visitors detouring from the Camel Trail along the valley bottom: they, like hikers, approach on a path through the vines.

Bob, Annie and Sam Lindo welcome some 30,000 visitors a year. Their tasting room opens on to a broad terrace overlooking the vines, and the product of the grapes below is poured in tasting samples, as half or full glasses, or sold by the bottle. It's a place to sit and sip in

Camel Valley's south-facing vineyards, seen from the opposite side of the valley. CAMEL VALLEY WINES

Vineyard cycle racks for visitors who follow the Camel Trail. AUTHOR

the sun, above the south-facing slope whose warmth, unusual even in gentle Cornwall, prompted Bob Lindo to plant vines in the first place.

That hadn't been a long-determined choice; rather, quite literally, it was linked to an accident. He and Annie had bought 33-hectare Little Denby Farm in 1982, well in advance of his planned retirement from the RAF, where he had reached the rank of squadron leader. They chose Cornwall because land was cheap, and thought probably they would continue keeping sheep and cattle. So much for look-ahead planning. When a devastating mid-air crash in 1986 left Lindo with severe spinal injuries, he was invalided out of his career as a pilot, spent months in rehabilitation and in 1987 became a full-time farmer.

He quickly realized just how warm that field below the farmhouse was – each summer the grass

turned brown – so why not try vines, 'just for fun'? In 1989, he and Annie planted eight thousand (there are four times that number now) entirely by hand, the beginning of a venture whose success is evidenced on the loaded shelves of the trophy cabinet alongside the Camel Valley tasting bar. The awards – trophies, bests-in-class and medals of every hue – don't come only from UK-based competitions, prestigious as the International Wine Challenge and the Decanter World Wine Awards are. Many have been won in worldwide sparkling-wine championships.

Camel Valley, at 10 hectares, is Cornwall's biggest vineyard and its from-the-beginning production total hit 1 million bottles in 2008. On the traditional English wine scale that's a sizeable operation, though against the new big investors it's tiny. There is no City profit behind the business, no massive bank loans. Bob Lindo is immensely proud of the fact that Camel Valley has been built up as a result of its own success. When money is made, it goes back into upgrading equipment, creating better visitor facilities, improving existing buildings or constructing new ones. It has allowed forward-thinking son Sam – in charge of winemaking and garlanded with English winemaker of the year accolades – to go ahead with what the family calls a 'shed to end all sheds'. That, explains his father, provides the kind of storage space more usually seen in champagne cellars, giving a reserve against inevitable vintage fluctuations. It's an example of how the family works together yet separately, with acceptance of each other's ideas rather than argument.

Thus it is Annie Lindo who makes all the decisions about Annie's Vineyard, the seyval blanc vines that lie immediately below the tasting terrace and are the source of Annie's Anniversary, surely the most personal of all English sparkling wines. Annie alone has tended the

vineyard since its planting, and Sam created the wine to mark the 100,000th time she'd pruned a vine, the millionth cut she'd made by hand with secateurs and her twentieth vintage.

The tackle-and-sort-any-problem-yourself approach startles some recruits to the small staff team. Bob Lindo smiles as he recalls the surprise of a new winemaking assistant when he learned he was expected to fix himself the piece of kit that had just gone wrong – but that's how Camel Valley works. There is plenty of sensible 'greenness', too, as solar panels generate all the electricity needed, with some left over to sell to the national grid, and grape waste is fed to dairy cows (before fermentation, of course, or they'd be rather too happy creatures).

Sparkling wine has become the main focus, with seyval blanc remaining alongside newer plantings of chardonnay and pinot noir and retaining its place as a major component of the flagship Cornwall Brut. All the sparkling wines are vintage, a deliberate decision. 'I want every year to be a memory of what the year was. I don't want a homogenous product,' is Bob Lindo's reasoning. Similarly, he doesn't want to ape champagne. 'The challenge is to make a different wine, and you can now.'

Bacchus is the still star, and Lindo had, just before the Brexit negotiations overtook smaller matters, persuaded the EU wine authorities to accept the Darnibole vineyard, where the bacchus ripens at unusually high sugar levels, as being sufficiently special to be given protected designation of origin status (PDO). In fact, the EU went further than he asked, including much more of Camel Valley's vineyard area in the Darnibole PDO, which could open up further individual quality labelling opportunities for the wines.

Discussion of such designation, though, is rather too technical for most of those who would rather simply enjoy the year-round tasting opportunities, summer tours and the chance to sip in the sun. Should visitors be tempted to remain for longer, Camel Valley is one of a number of English vineyards with on-site accommo-

Darnibole bacchus vines, on a very special site. CAMEL VALLEY WINES

dation. At the two cottages available for weekly rental, the Lindos are now welcoming the sons and daughters of those who stayed in the early days. Day visitors, too, return regularly. The bicycles parked in the rack when I was there belonged to a young couple from the Midlands who frequently holiday at Padstow and each time head along the Camel Trail to the vineyard. That's good for future business, Bob Lindo predicts: 'There's no doubt which wine they'll choose for their wedding, and then for the christenings. . .'

Leventhorpe Vineyard, within the city boundary of Leeds, Yorkshire: the warm north

Right at the very opposite end of England's wine lands from Camel Valley lies the 2-hectare vineyard that George and Janet Bowden established in 1985, not far from where the Cisterican monks of twelfth-century Kirkstall Abbey most likely had their vine plots. When I met George Bowden at the English Wine Producers' May 2017 trade and press tasting, just about every other grower there was reporting damage, quite often severe damage, from the previous month's wicked air frost. 'Not a bud touched,' he told me.

That fits with his experience when he first saw the Leventhorpe site. There was snow everywhere, except on one south-facing field that was basking in sun. Even so far north, even before much sign of warmer growing seasons, it was the perfect place for vines. A light, quick-draining sandy loam soil lies above cracked sandstone, warming rapidly in spring, and there are both protective trees and water (the River Aire, the Aire and Calder Navigation canal, and a series of small lakes) all around. The grapes ripen well and yield generously, so Bowden rarely chaptalizes his madeleine angevine and needs to add only a very little sugar to the seyval blanc. Even in 2012, when the results from most of southern England's vineyards were dire, Leventhorpe's bottles were winning gold and silver medals. The wines are distinctive, remarkably aromatic and – the seyval especially – even more characterful and expressive after an extra year or so in bottle. There should, their maker argues, be a law against selling English wine too soon.

George Bowden and the pride of Yorkshire.
LEVENTHORPE VINEYARD

George Bowden has long had a serious interest in wine – to explain how that came about would take an impossible amount of time, he told me. His non-wine professional background is as a chemist and geologist, and expertise in both has contributed to his success in growing vines successfully and making good wine. 'Land dictates the wine,' he emphasized, launching into a comparison between his site and the finest in Burgundy. When our discussion moved to winemaking, it quickly became far too technical for inclusion here. But he summed up his approach very simply: 'There is no point in making wine in Yorkshire unless you make the quality.' And he insists that this philosophy should apply throughout the UK.

Far from everything about Leventhorpe is dourly scientific and serious. Bowden takes great delight in recounting how one of his customers, a former coach with the French rugby union squad, introduced his colleagues in Les Bleus to the Yorkshire product. Tasting it blind, they thought it must come from the south-west of France. If the French won the World Cup, suggested the ex-coach, they would be rewarded with Leventhorpe madeleine angevine, while if they lost they would have to make do with French wine. The motto on the Leventhorpe labels, 'pretium victoriae' also reflects George Bowden's sense of fun. The words translate literally from the Latin as 'the price of victory'. They were reputedly used, so the story goes, by Roman general (and later emperor) Vespasian as he stalked out of the senate hearing after successfully defending himself against indictment for spending too heavily – notably on the use of elephants – during the campaign to conquer Britain. Bowden is at pains to argue, however, that much more appropriate than the literal translation is his preferred 'worth the effort': a sentiment that might well, he suggests, be relevant for much of England's wine.

Such special characters apart, there are others in the UK wine industry who put their individual mark on their wines in another way, by making them according to very personal principles.

Davenport Vineyards, near Rotherfield, East Sussex: where organic is right for the next generation

'I'd always wanted to do it,' was Will Davenport's response when I asked why he had committed to organic vine-growing and winemaking. 'This is the place where my kids are brought up.' When he planted vines in the early 1990s on a little over a hectare of land previously grazed by dairy cows at Limney Farm, on the East Sussex/Kent border, he didn't completely eschew chemicals, but that changed in 2001. He hoped the greener approach would succeed – 'I would have dumped it if it didn't' – and he was helped by the conviction of a German consultant who assured him that, if his soil was properly balanced and rich in the natural bacteria that swallow up mildew spores, all would work well. The alternative was to use vast quantities of chemicals to tackle botrytis, for which he could find no environmentally friendlier control. The strategy worked. 'My biggest worry was that the vines would just get wiped out by mildew, but that has not proved a problem at all.'

Davenport's wines are highly respected among fellow professionals, and not simply because they are organic. Consumers like them too, meeting them mostly in restaurants, though there are some direct sales via the website and the local Waitrose. 'Organic helps – it gets

Will Davenport: 'There is no point in selling rubbish and saying it is organic.' AUTHOR

people interested in looking at the wine,' their maker says. But it has to be good: 'There's no point in selling rubbish wine and saying it is organic.' As most sales are through the trade, his income per bottle is much less than those who sell at the cellar door receive, but then he doesn't have to provide a smart public-welcoming façade to the warren of former dairy buildings that house his winery.

With a total of 10 hectares of vines, all grown according to the same green ethos, divided between Limney Farm and his parents' farm in Kent, Davenport is probably the largest UK organic producer, but quality is more important than quantity, he insists. He aims for the best possible grapes, that he can largely 'leave as nature intended' in the winery. 'If you need a lot of intervention, that means you haven't got good grapes.' In both vineyards and winery he works generally to Soil Association standards, which set lower limits of sulphur, for example, than the EU organic rules. Much effort goes into soil improvement, with huge amounts of green-waste compost applied in the vineyard. If there is a powdery mildew attack, he picks off affected leaves into a bin bag and disposes of them, or uses a little sulphur for prevention and potassium bicarbonate for control. Nettle and comfrey infusions also help the vines resist disease. The wines are fermented using natural yeasts, organic sugar is used if alcohol levels need boosting, minimal fining and filtering is practised, and there is 'no GM anything'. What Davenport does is 'part science, part intuition', but it is always methodical. 'You've got to be more on the ball than a non-organic person.'

Davenport's commitment goes beyond the actual growing and making. The whole operation is close to being carbon neutral, with surplus electricity from solar panels offsetting the diesel needed to fuel his tractors. He doesn't heat his winery in winter and limits its summer temperature with an evaporative cooler that sucks air through a wet cardboard membrane; cool England, he points out, needs much less energy expended on summer temperature control than most other wine-producing countries. His wine goes into lightweight bottles, saving nearly 2 tonnes of glass a year without the people pouring his wines even noticing the weight difference. 'That makes complete sense – they do the job, look the same and I feel better.' Yet he believes no other UK winery follows his example.

At Limney Farm, pinot noir and auxerrois, an Alsace variety rarely seen in England, grow in 60 centimetres of loam overlying iron-rich sandstone on a steep, west-facing slope, their grapes destined for white and rosé sparkling wine. Average yields in East Sussex are much lower than at the warmer Kent sites, where he has the three champagne varieties for more sparkling wine, plus extra pinot noir for still wines. There, too, are the very first vines he planted, in 1991, the germanic varieties – bacchus, ortega, siegerrebe, faberrebe and huxelrebe – which make up the aromatic, refreshing Horsmonden dry white that demonstrates why these grapes still firmly deserve their place on England's wine list.

Albury Organic Vineyard, near Guildford, Surrey: a schoolboy dream comes of age

On the North Downs in Surrey, a more recent organic enterprise is the realization of Nick Wenman's long-held dream, a dream revealed in his pre-legal-drinking-age schooldays. He perturbed his headmaster more than a little by choosing as his economics prize book *The World Atlas of Wine*. 'When I retired, what else could I do. . . ,' he says today.

That early retirement, from IT, came in 2006. Within two years, Wenman had negotiated a long lease on an ideally located site and was ready to plant. The Surrey hills site was a fortuitous choice, for recent research indicates that vines were grown there in the 1640s: the rows running down to a lake shown on a contemporary etching are near identical to the eighteenth-century Painshill Park layout. John Evelyn also mentioned the vines, in a 1670 diary entry. From the beginning, Wenman's intention was to reject a chemical-based approach. 'Organic felt right. I decided I had to do it to start with, otherwise I would never do it.' His mentor was Will Davenport; his advisor, Stephen Skelton, 'tried

Nick Wenman:
'Organic felt right.'
JOHN POWELL/ALBURY
ORGANIC VINEYARD

really hard' to convince him that organic was not the best way to go (yet Skelton accepted his client's doggedness, and continued his consultancy).

Beyond a gut feeling that the green approach is good for the planet, Wenman does admit to a more mercenary incentive. There should be, he feels, a niche market for organic English wine and, like Davenport, he believes that making it does attract extra attention. A decade on, he is well aware of the difficulties and acknowledges his own 'extreme' naivety at the beginning: 'I completely underestimated the amount of work and money required.' Most of Albury's 5 hectares of vines are the champagne varieties, plus a little seyval blanc and an even tinier quantity of pinot gris. The intention has always been to focus largely on sparkling wine, although the still Silent Pool rosé has gained a cult following after being chosen as one of the wines served on the Royal Barge in the 2012 Jubilee River Thames parade. There is the potential, in time, to double the vineyard size.

Following the organic route makes sustainability of yield an even bigger issue than it is for conventional growers, Wenman says. 'Yields are definitely lower, possibly by fifteen to twenty per cent, because of being

organic.' But, whatever the growing principles, the major cause of yield variation is weather, and the 2017 late-April air frost was a cruel reminder of how much a single night of temperatures falling below minus 2 degrees celsius can severely reduce the year's potential harvest. The new growth on 80 per cent of Albury's vines was badly damaged. It was one of the hardest moments in Wenman's vine-growing experience, but he is steadfast: 'We won't give up!'

Weather apart, one problem in the vineyard is management of weeds: young vines especially find the competition unwelcome. Spreading thick layers of wood chips is the solution. Another issue is disease control. The vineyard's seyval blanc in particular is too often hit by botrytis, though powdery mildew is rare. Wenman uses minimum quantities of copper and sulphur, and is hopeful that a bark-based alternative to the former will gain EU approval. Biodynamic sprays are also in the programme. 'We just have to be on the ball all the time.'

He points out that in the UK all vines are affected by the limited time between harvest and leaf fall, leaving little opportunity for the plants to build up reserves for the following year: another reason for low grape yields.

Healthy pinot meunier bud at Albury. ALBURY ORGANIC VINEYARD

Yet green harvesting – removing some bunches to give those remaining a chance to ripen better – is a regular, necessary practice at many vineyards, including Albury.

In years when their crop is particularly poor, organic growers don't have a potential escape route that is open to those less concerned about chemicals, Wenman adds. There are no organic grapes that can be bought in to supplement their own harvests.

Albury's vineyard manager, Alex Valsecchi, had viticultural experience from her native Italy and from New Zealand before moving to England and the Royal Horticultural Society Wisley garden, where the vineyard, and the rest of the fruit, was her responsibility. She is chalk to Wenman's cheese. She was, he grins, nicknamed Chemical Allie when she arrived at Albury. 'Am I convinced about organic growing? No! But fundamentally anything can be done if you are willing to do it and to do it properly,' she told me. 'Do I like the results? Of course I do.' As does her family in Italy, who happily drink the Albury rosé she regularly takes home. 'It's definitely a challenge to grow vines in this country, but wherever you grow vines you force them

to do something they don't want to do naturally. But we are not here to produce a barolo or an amarone. We are here to produce sparkling wine.'

The last stages of that process are the responsibility of the Litmus Wines team, close by at Denbies, where the winery is one of the few in the UK to comply with the EU rules for organic winemaking. These insist that yeasts and sugar must be organic, specify permitted stabilization materials and set lower limits on sulphites, sugar and de-acidification. The rules were introduced in 2013, ending the rather odd situation in which, Europe-wide, wines could be labelled only as 'made from organic grapes', not more straightforwardly 'organic'. Wenman doesn't feel confident to do his own winemaking, even if he had the cash to build and equip a winery, and he is happy with the Litmus arrangement. 'We are involved in every major step of the process.' With champagne specialist Matthieu Elzinga, one of the three Litmus partners, monitoring the ripening grapes and advising on harvest times as well as producing the final bottles, 'it's almost as good as having your own winemaker'.

Kristin Syltevik and the green, green grass of Oxney.
AUTHOR

Oxney Organic Estate, near Rye, East Sussex: green expression of PR

There's a particular memory I have of my early spring visit to Oxney: the near-croquet-lawn perfection of the grass between the rows of hard-pruned vines. That green image perfectly expressed the spirit of the 8.5-hectare vineyard, part of a very much larger mixed farm bought by Norwegian-born Kristin Syltevik, who had worked in top-end public relations, and her partner Paul Dobson, a former golf professional, in 2009.

The estate, all run organically, is on the East Sussex/ Kent border, overlooking the Isle of Oxney in the River Rother valley. There are pedigree sheep, arable fields, swathes of wildflowers, winter-flooded meadows that attract migrating birds, coppiced woodland and, of course, the vines. The barns that Syltevik has converted into three holiday cottages echo the overall sustainability theme, with heating from the estate wood-chip burner and power from renewably sourced electricity, and two shepherds' huts in the vineyard provide further atmospheric accommodation. People love the place and local volunteers work in the vineyard, where one block has been named after an exceptionally loyal helper.

The 32,000-plus vines, chardonnay, pinots noir and meunier and a little seyval, were planted from 2012 to 2014, a good proportion by hand. Everything happens on the spot, with a small but perfect winery inside a former oast house, where winemaker Ben Smith and consultant winemaker David Cowderoy have crafted much-admired wines – the second vintage pinot noir rosé was named best still rosé in the 2016 English and Welsh Wine of the Year competition. The first classic blend sparkling wine was released in late 2016.

Why, I asked Kristin Syltevik, change career in such a fundamental way? Not one reason but many, she replied. She welcomed the challenge to learn something entirely new. She and Dobson had the land, and she could see its potential. Working organically fitted with her own convictions. She relishes the closeness to consumers. Most tellingly: 'It is lovely that people have such a pleasure from what you have done.'

The new life isn't easy, with Oxney's vines facing the inevitable risks: frost, hungry wildlife (fencing keeps out rabbits and deer but not badgers) and fungal diseases. To

Oxney's winery, a converted oast house nestled in the vines. GONEWILD/OXNEY ORGANIC ESTATE

combat the last, she makes her own preventative nettle and comfrey infusion and also uses a garlic and citrus mix, plus bacteria to attack botrytis. Sulphur and copper treatments are kept to minimal levels, more biodynamic than organic, and spraying is precise. She sees all the effort rewarded as the grapes are pressed, with the results different from each clone, each plot. Her enthusiasm is infectious when she describes the fine blanc de blancs anticipated from one champagne clone of chardonnay that flourishes particularly well at Oxney.

One other pleasure, which didn't always exist in the PR world, is the friendliness of her newly chosen business community and its willingness to help a newcomer. Just a short while before I visited Oxney, she had gratefully accepted the loan of an essential item of winery equipment when her own broke down.

These three organic growers are among the bigger followers of the anti-chemical route. But they're very small fry compared to the UK's major wine producers.

Chapel Down, Kent: the biggest of all

No other UK wine producer yet reaches close to the 700,000-bottles-a-year total of Chapel Down, but what the warmly welcomed wine tourists see there is quite a modest affair. There is, naturally, loads of wine on the shop shelves (plus beers – Chapel Down also has a brewery – and other goodies), a restaurant where I had what was definitely the best meal of my vineyards-of-England tour, and a smart new view-over-the-vines tasting room. But the scale of the place is not at all overwhelming. Even the surrounding vineyards are quite limited in area. They include Spots Farm, the 2.33-hectare plot planted by Stephen Skelton in 1977. Then, the farm had just been bought by Skelton's father-in-law and, given its closeness to sea level, good light soil and shelter-providing hedges, was thought to be an excellent site for vines. And so it was, proved when 1980 Spots Farm seyval blanc, only the second vintage, took the English Wine of the Year title in

Spots Farm, the first vineyard planted by Stephen Skelton, now part of Chapel Down. AUTHOR

1981. Skelton sold the vineyard and winery in 1986, though he continued to make the wines, but another nine years were to pass before before Chapel Down moved in.

That modest area of vines at Tenterden, 10 hectares, is only a taster. Chapel Down has extensive vineyards elsewhere, including the prime Kit's Coty site on the North Downs chalk. This is the source of Coeur de Cuvée 2013 blanc de blancs, which raised eyebrows throughout the industry when the 1,600 bottles went on sale for £99.99 each on St George's Day 2017, topping the price of England's previously most expensive sparkling wine by £25. The grapes from the 80 hectares planted in north Kent fill two articulated lorries every day during harvest time, and fruit from a further 60 hectares will add to those loads. More new vineyards will join these as suitable sites

are found. Chapel Down also has long-term contracts with other grape-growers, in Kent, Essex and Sussex. With its own vineyards, there are well over twenty locations from which the fruit comes. Head winemaker Josh Donaghay-Spire and his colleagues watch over all the vineyards, advising the growers, aiming for quality and avoiding problems that might mean the rejection of any part of the crop. In addition, further supplies of grapes are bought on the 'spot' market, from non-contracted growers, sometimes from as distant as Dorset. By 2023 Chapel Down intends to produce 1.4 million bottles a year.

That scale makes Donaghay-Spire go to work with a smile on his face. Provided he delivers the regular goods – 'we cannot run out of some wines, like the brut non-vintage, as it's in all the big supermarkets' – he has room to experiment. 'Standard wines are all very well, but we have less credibility as winemakers if we are not pushing the boundaries, particularly at this nascent stage of the industry.' So he can make six different wines from bacchus grapes, for example. He can try out skin contact in white wines, use wild yeasts for fermentation, make small batches of wines from unusual grapes such as albariño, even venture into orange wine. 'We have to keep things interesting for us and for consumers. And the lessons from these wines will trickle down into large-volume wines.'

Since he arrived at Chapel Down in 2010, Donaghay-Spire, another of the highly skilled Plumpton College graduates, has made a clear mark on the wines. He isn't a fan of high-acid results, so almost all go through malolactic conversion, allowing a lower dosage (the addition of sugar in the final top-up liquid) in the sparkling wines. He has reduced levels of preservative sulphur, arguing that English wines aren't intended to live for decades, and has also significantly increased the use of oak barrels in the winery.

Production is split roughly half-and-half between still and sparkling, with bacchus the most important grape in the former. But that is the only germanic cross in the planting plans. Instead, the emphasis is on chardonnay, pinot noir, pinot meunier and pinot blanc. Though there are non-vintage sparkling wines, most bottles carry the year of harvest: 'We have to celebrate vintage differences.' Those differences do cause difficulties, however. In wet 2012, for example, none of the top-of-the-range wine was made; instead, the limited amount of fruit that could be harvested from those best vineyards went into the wines that Chapel Down needed for its big, regular customers.

Does he see a global warming effect, good or bad, I asked Donaghay-Spire. 'Possibly the ripening season is earlier, there is lower acidity, higher sugars, which are all to the good,' he replied. But most if not all of that could be due as much to the better professional understanding and skill of those now growing grapes in the UK, he added. 'There have been major leaps in site selection, clonal selection, varietal selection.'

Donaghay-Spire has overseen the move of some of the operation from the Tenterden base to a new warehouse and distribution centre at Ashford, where the riddling and disgorging of the sparkling wines also takes place. It saves a lot of articulated lorry movement on narrow Kent roads and has freed up space for expanding the Tenterden winery. There is, he adds, an engineering side to his work: 'They didn't teach me that at Plumpton. Here, you have to turn your hand to everything.'

Even if Chapel Down is big in wine terms, with fifty full-time employees, it is hardly a large-scale business in the broader world. It does, though, innovate way beyond normal wine business practices. In September 2014 it was the first publicly listed company to offer shares through equity crowd-funding. Not only did the initiative bring in almost £4 million, to help expand the vineyard area, but it also attracted close to 1,500 new shareholders. As long as they hold their shares, they receive a substantial discount on Chapel Down wines. But more important to Donaghay-Spire is their role as ambassadors. 'They have bought into the brand, they buy, they tell the story.'

The story is spread, too, by the 40,000 people who visit Tenterden each year and taste the wines. The man who makes them is keen that more and more should come. 'I want Chapel Down to be the opposite of those exclusive champagne cellars where you have to call and might get an appointment if you are lucky. We are all about inclusivity, bringing people here, showing them how wine is made, why this bottle costs more than that bottle, making a connection with them that they take away.'

Josh Donaghay-Spire in the Chapel Down winery. CHAPEL DOWN

Denbies Wine Estate, Dorking, Surrey: on a grand scale

But for the unusual uniformity of its rows of green plants, Denbies could strike the uninitiated visitor more as a large-scale garden centre than a vineyard. Go through the front entrance of the imposing building, turn right and the 'garden centre' experience continues: a big and broadly stocked shop, a bright café beneath an atrium, a gallery displaying local artists' work, upstairs a restaurant with a fine view. Outside, paths lead to a farm shop, an area selling plants, even a bed and breakfast lined up for conversion to a boutique hotel. Chief executive officer Chris White makes no excuse for all this. More than that, he celebrates the large-scale leisure experience open to all. It is intended to bring Denbies wines before as many people as possible, as well as providing income – close to half the business's total – to help sustain what for three decades has been England's largest single-site wine estate.

Certainly, Denbies can take credit for introducing a very large number of consumers to English wine, particularly through the own-label bottles it supplies to supermarkets. 'Some people are snooty about that, but we think it is very important. It gives people a much wider access to English wine and through economies of scale we can guarantee quality and consistency,' White told me.

There is, as well, plenty of wine-associated activity for the 350,000 visitors who arrive each year. An extensive programme offers vineyard tours in a tourist train or a horse-drawn carriage, tasting in the atmospheric cellars, visits to the winery, food and wine matching, day-long wine workshops, sessions combining cheese-making and winemaking, and much more. September sees the annual Bacchus Marathon, while in October there is a chance to join in the harvest. The indoor tours take in a film that celebrates the thirty years of Denbies (very informative and a cut above many winery videos); outside, there are options to add a glass of fizz en route through the vines. With all these opportunities, my wine-educator tour guide Victor Maguire pointed out, thousands of the visitors leave with an understanding of the basics of grape-growing, winemaking and the story of English wine. Others simply enjoy walking on the 11 kilometres of footpaths that run through the vines and the extensive woodland surrounding them. Or they come to Denbies as wedding guests or to attend a variety of functions, from murder mystery evenings to tea dances.

Denbies, introducing English wine to a wide audience.
DENBIES WINE ESTATE

The cellar at Denbies, an atmospheric setting for tastings. DENBIES WINE ESTATE

A green sea: Denbies vineyard. HELEN DIXON/DENBIES WINE ESTATE

There is a lengthy agricultural history to today's vineyard, whose name comes from John Denby, who farmed the land in the sixteenth century. By the 1850s, the owner was builder Thomas Cubitt, whose construction legacy includes much of Belgravia in central London, Osborne House on the Isle of Wight and part of Buckingham Palace. The 100-room Italianate mansion he built on his huge new Surrey estate does not survive, however: it was demolished in 1953, and much of the land was split up and sold. Some 250 hectares, though, remained in the hands of Cubitt's descendants until 1984, when it was bought by Adrian White, chairman of a major water-treatment company and Chris's father. He had intended to run the land as a conventional farm, but that didn't make business sense (some parts sloped so much that combine harvesters had to creep across with crab-like sideways caution), so an alternative use was needed. Felicitously, there was an expert on hand. From his home in Dorking, consultant geologist Richard Selley looked out over White's land. He realized how suitable it would be for a vineyard. 'Just for a joke, I thought I would write a little consulting paper just as I would for an oil company or similar business,' he explains in the *A Year in the Vineyard* film that is shown to visitors. Little did he anticipate the result. Nor perhaps, looking back rather further, would Adrian White's father, a strict teetotaller, have appreciated the wine-producing route his son and grandson decided to follow.

From the first planting of just over a hectare in 1986, Denbies' vineyard has grown almost a hundred-fold, with a little more expansion planned. Only Rathfinny, when fully planted, is in line to overtake it as the UK's largest single-site vineyard. A silty clay loam soil overlies chalk, and there is shelter from much of the prevailing wind. From the beginning, noble grape varieties were chosen alongside the germanic crosses, the likes of riesling, pinot blanc, pinot noir and chardonnay, and the experimentation continues. Denbies was the first English winery to bottle sauvignon blanc, it is championing the new solaris variety, it has released a zero-dosage (no added sugar) blanc de blancs sparkling wine, and in favourable vintages it makes a super-premium dessert wine from late-harvest ortega.

Denbies has the only mechanical harvester in the UK. DENBIES WINE ESTATE

Though Denbies' own production is huge, grapes are bought in from other vineyards in the south-east, to meet a growing demand and also because, as Chris White says, 'we don't want to have all our eggs in one basket'. He admits that success can have a downside – in 2013 the company was 'really strapped for wine' because so much had been drunk during the 2012 London Olympics and Royal Jubilee celebrations, leaving reserves too low. But with an average production now of 450,000 bottles a year, that problem shouldn't occur again.

There is serious investment in the winery and outside. Denbies is the first UK vineyard to bring in a mechanical harvesting machine, which speeds up the picking process. The estate is also pioneering the use of the frost-busting Tow and Blow moveable fan that towers over the vines, though unfortunately even that level of technology couldn't counteract the severe air frost of late April 2017. A new minimal pruning technique is practised on müller-thurgau vines planted on lower-lying land, which, if frost doesn't cause problems, brings a fine harvest. Herbicides are no longer part of the chemical armoury, in an increasing commitment towards greener practices in the vineyard. The winery operates to EU organic standards, as its contract wine-making customers include organic vineyards.

Chris White is justifiably proud of how much Denbies can spread the word about English wine to consumers who previously knew little about it. 'When people leave here after the tour they have a much greater appreciation of what goes into their bottle of wine. They see how much investment and time goes in. They're sold on it.'

Lyme Bay Winery, near Axminster, Devon: much more liquid than wine alone

Lyme Bay is a place with, unusually, no vineyards within sight. But among UK wineries Lyme Bay is a very unusual set-up in a number of ways. It's a non-stop operation, its 350,000-litre-capacity tanks in busy use all year round. They contain more besides the juice of English wine grapes, however. The day I was there plastic picnic goblets were being filled with Spanish red for supermarket customers, cider was fermenting and a team was out picking young nettle leaves for the kind of country wine you'd expect to be made in a WI member's kitchen. What is a talented Plumpton wine graduate whose experience stretches as far as France, California and Australia doing here?

In 2015 Liam Idzikowski was headhunted by his friend James Lambert, managing director of the expanding company that began life as a cider producer. Lyme Bay founder Nigel Howard, a London banker, had initially simply wanted to move away from the city, but his rustic dream has developed into a highly sophisticated operation, even though it is set deep in the east Devon countryside. By the mid-2000s he had realized that making wine could fit very well into his successful, broader-than-cider drinks company. In 2009 and 2010, 26,000 vines were planted on two sites totalling 7 hectares 'within a stone's throw' of the winery. From the outset, the English wine initiative has had to be a properly commercial addition to the business, needing to pay its way or face abandonment. To achieve that, it needs a very much larger quantity of grapes than those two vineyards can provide. The extra fruit is sourced from other growers, some as far away as Essex, but the transport operation is well organized, with grapes in the winery and pressed within twelve hours of picking.

To Idzikowski, buying in grapes from carefully selected and monitored growers makes a lot of sense. 'For us it's all about consistency and quality. Probably the best way in England is not to depend on one site.' Diversity of origin brings extra dimensions to the wines, with a blend of very aromatic but somewhat green bacchus from Devon with riper Essex grapes, for example, resulting in a wine with far more character than ones made from the individual components alone.

Idzikowski is in charge of all the half-million litres of liquids produced each year by Lyme Bay, but his greatest enthusiasm is clearly for the English wine and the opportunities he has with such a broad terroir tapestry of grapes. He showed me an immensely

promising pinot noir, ageing gently in barrel, from grapes grown in Essex. Unlike the Lyme Bay Shoreline blend or the own-label wines (the National Trust is one customer), that pinot will never be a large-production wine, so there is small-scale as well as large-scale potential for his skills. He is a great fan of fruit from Essex, where growing-season temperature averages close to 1 degree celsius above that in Devon. 'It's one of my favourite places for grape-growing, but it will never become as fashionable as Kent.' The Garden

of England is more likely to become the Bordeaux of England, he predicts.

Beyond believing in the necessity of good grapes, Idzikowski is an avid user of technical advances to aid winemaking; he believes they are invaluable in a big-volume operation. He is proud of the winery's well-equipped laboratory where there is, for example, a piece of kit that can measure the oxygen level in a filled, sealed bottle of wine – particularly useful when checking samples.

Big as Lyme Bay Winery is compared to most of its grape-wine-only compatriots, it is very welcoming to visitors, who can buy its products, and other local edible temptations, in the well-stocked shop. The stainless steel tanks are clearly visible behind the counter, and here's an intriguing thought for buyers of Shoreline or pinot noir rosé, or any of the other wines: the tank in which it was made might a short time earlier have held mead or country wine. With impeccable cleaning in between, of course.

Bolney Wine Estate, near Haywards Heath, East Sussex: red is big and even bubbly

England isn't big on red wines, but Bolney produces more than any other winery, and the results are impressive. Much of the success is down to location – the vines are planted in a warm, very sheltered hollow below the lip of the South Downs, where heat-retaining sandstone lies beneath the sandy/loam or clay topsoil. It was once a chicken farm, but in 1969 Rodney and Janet Pratt saw its potential for the vineyard they wanted to create. Their first planting in 1972 was of only a little more than a hectare, but over the years the area under vines has grown almost sixteen-fold, and a new winery is allowing production to expand to 300,000 bottles a year. It remains a family business, with the Pratts' daughter Sam Linter in charge of winemaking, and Sam's daughter Charlotte also involved, though in a media rather than winery role. Clearly, Bolney is another multi-generation English wine business.

As is the case in so many longer-established vine-

Sam Linter and the Bolney vines. GRAEME ROBERTSON/BOLNEY WINE ESTATE

yards, the choice of varieties has changed, with more concentration on familiar international grapes than on the germanic crosses. Some of the latter are still favoured, however, with new plantings of bacchus producing a splendidly clean and aromatic wine, while some of the would-be advances have proved premature. Even a warm English spot wasn't right for merlot, as Sam Linter found – the young chardonnay vines that visitors see from the café terrace replace that particular experiment.

Pinot noir has long ripened well here, and has contributed much to Bolney's red reputation, with successive vintages taking silver medals in the 2015, 2016 and 2017 International Wine Challenge. Rondo and dornfelder are planted, too, the latter appearing in the unusual guise of a traditional-method red fizz

Ready for reds: grape harvest at Bolney. GRAEME ROBERTSON/BOLNEY WINE ESTATE

that spends a year on its lees. Unlike sweet new world sparkling syrah, it's a dry wine, though full of dark summer fruits, which its makers like to drink with cold meats. All three red varieties go into a rosé that evokes strawberries all the way through, from colour to scent to flavour. A series of medal-winning sparkling cuvées combine the classic champagne grapes, and the dry still pinot gris regularly sells out before the next vintage is ready; the 2016 carried off two trophies in the inaugural UK Wine Awards and helped Bolney win the title of winery of the year.

Bolney epitomizes a lot of what is so good about English wine now. Most crucially, the product is excellent, but there is much more. Considerable effort goes into wine tourism, and the experience is welcoming and enjoyably educational. I remember how impressed I was the first time I did the tour – it was a very effective explanation of how grapes are grown and turned into wine, comprehensive yet easily understandable – and a repeat experience ten years on was just as good. Things have advanced in terms of space and facilities, including the inviting first-floor café with its terrace overlooking the vines, but the guide's wine knowledge was as formidable and well presented as before. For the paying customers (fortunately for the future of English wine, most I met were in their twenties and thirties) the tour demonstrated very clearly how much care and effort goes into the making of both still and sparkling wine in England – and by the end of the visit they appreciated how the price necessarily reflects that. Maybe, one couple said, to nods from others, English wine still wouldn't be their everyday supper wine, but for a celebration or to accompany a special meal with friends they'd put it at the top of their to-buy list. Spread that attitude through the whole UK wine-buying public, and sales will soar.

Among the UK's modern vignerons there are plenty whose previous careers are invaluable in their new one. It's rather different from the days when the 'retirement project' vineyards, set up with minimal knowledge or understanding, were too often the norm. As Kit Lindlar, the doyen of English sparkling wine advisors, once said, the only qualifications required to set up a winery were 'a Major's pension and a double-barrelled surname'.

The pebbles at Pebblebed. AUTHOR

Pebblebed Vineyards, close to Exeter, Devon: a local product for local sale

Geoff Bowen, formerly a geologist specializing in ground water assessments, is one who can put previous professional expertise to good use, identifying sites that have the right potential for vine-growing, from the roots down at least. Pebblebed is more than a pretty name for a wine business. It also expresses the vineyard geology, as does a small display intended for visitors. Along the edge of the winery wall, almost like a flower bed, sits a narrow patch of pebbles, rounded from underwater movement. They are from a unique local geological feature, the Budleigh Salterton pebblebeds, laid down

Sheep among young Pebblebed vines. AUTHOR

by a huge river system 200 million years ago, which appear on the modern soil surface in outcrops close to the vines.

But this wine story is rooted in something other than geology and south Devon's temperate climate. Those factors were not its prompting. Quite simply, there was the need to find some practical use for an area of south-facing land that came with a house that one of Bowen's friends had bought. Vines, said Bowen, and a community vineyard came into being, with ten families chipping in £100 each to pay for the planting of a couple of thousand square metres. Almost twenty years on that vineyard is one among several: the Pebblebed vines cover 10 hectares and average a production of 50,000 bottles a year, half still wine, half sparkling. Ambition is limited, in a rather particular and commendably green way, to 'produce a local product for local sale'. Bowen is very reluctant indeed to sell beyond a 15-kilometre radius of Exeter, and his USP is simple: 'Exeter's own wine'.

Rather a lot is consumed even closer to the vines. Part of the Pebblebed operation is a wine bar in riverside Topsham, a mere 3 kilometres from the winery, where there are opportunities to taste and drink alongside simple but tasty food, an ideal combination. Beyond that, the wines are popular for corporate events in and around Exeter.

The varieties that do best in south Devon's warm but rather wet climate are the germanic crosses, with seyval blanc enjoying the conditions most: 'It's bullet-proof. We have no need to use pesticides or fungicides on it.' Bowen has tried the champagne varieties, but they're not happy, and he would not choose them if he was planting anew. He largely follows organic growing practices. Why should he risk his own health, he argues, by being in the middle of a cloud of chemicals spraying out from the tractor he's driving? 'It's all about producing good wines, and if we can achieve quality with organic practice that's all to the good.'

And there is good generally in the home product. 'If you're thinking of a healthy wine it has to be English.' With an average alcohol content of 10.5 per cent, he points out, that means as much as a third less alcohol than in a 14 per cent hot-climate wine, and a third fewer calories.

Stopham Vineyard, near Pulborough, West Sussex: engineering skills introduced in the winery

If happy plants are responsible for a better-flavoured product, the vines that Simon Woodhead has planted on a south-facing 5.6-hectare slope in the South Downs National Park, with their roots in free-draining sandy soil, should produce fine wines. And they do. The site is low and sheltered, and the vines look down to the River Arun, gleaming in the sun. Around, there are mature trees, new hedgerows and long-planted ones, and grass growing between the rows of vines. The countryside is calm and quiet, raptors soar (their prevalence deters smaller birds with a taste for ripe grapes, valuable when yields are already low), and there is no pressure to replace the vines with any more intensive crop.

Woodhead's first visit to the site came at an opportune moment. He was studying vineyard establishment at Plumpton and had been invited to a friend's party at Stopham manor house. 'I saw all these sandy, empty fields. They ticked all the boxes.' Wine was to be a new career for the engineer who designed sensors for Formula One racing cars. McLaren had made him redundant; he had gone to Spain to learn the language, had become fascinated by the wine and was considering starting an import business. Hence the Plumpton course. But he decided he wanted to make wine rather than simply sell it. First, 'I had to find rich friends who had money to invest . . .'

His engineering background is another example of past career put to present use. It has prompted the creation of much bespoke equipment in the small winery (discussed in the previous chapter). Also, his childhood enthusiasm for gardening shows in the careful attention he and assistant winemaker Tom Bartlett pay to the vines. Measured end to end, the rows run for 26 kilometres: 'A lot to prune!' They are productive now, but the lack of natural nutrients in the soil meant

Stopham's vines look down to the River Arun and the South Downs beyond. AUTHOR

they were slow to establish. Manure from the cattle on the main Stopham farm, plus compost and fertilizer, encouraged them and continues to be necessary. The first were planted in 2007, with the aim from the beginning to make the best possible still white wines. A decade on, even with sparkling so predominant, only a tenth of Stopham's production bubbles. Pinot blanc and pinot gris, plus some bacchus, provide the still whites; dornfelder becomes rosé; and chardonnay, pinot noir and auxerrois go into the sparkling. To develop maximum sugar levels the grapes are left to ripen as late as possible, until cold or botrytis makes harvesting essential, and then comes Woodhead's inventive approach in the winery.

Visitors on pre-booked tours are very welcome at Stopham. It's an interesting place for any wine lover, and with Woodhead or Bartlett as guide, every question will receive an authoritative answer.

Polgoon Vineyard, Penzance, Cornwall: fishing for a land use

The previous career of Polgoon owners John and Kim Coulson may not have contributed much towards their wine initiative, but it is a story well worth sharing. Formerly fish merchants, they sold the business and invested in an old farmhouse to accommodate their growing family, planning to build holiday homes on some of the accompanying land. That didn't work out, so an alternative was needed. Various farming options were considered and rejected, until they met Bob Lindo of Camel Valley Vineyards. Vines it had to be and, like Stopham's, those at the top of the site have a splendid view, looking out over Mounts Bay to St Michael's Mount.

The Coulsons' first wine, from the 2006 harvest of pinot noir and rondo, took the best still rosé title in the UK Vineyard Association's annual wine of the year competition. Cheekily, it beat the entry from the Coulsons' Camel Valley mentor. But the soggy summers of 2007 and 2008 meant disaster for the grape harvests, so cidermaking – including cider created in the sparkling wine way, with second fermentation in bottle – was introduced to keep the business afloat. More recently, there has been further investment and kinder weather. Among new plantings, bacchus particularly has flourished, and there have been more awards for both still and the newer sparkling wines.

The vineyards that follow now don't group thematically, so be a happy, randomly wandering wine tourist and keep on reading. Several are away from the southern counties where vine concentration is strongest. Talk to their owners or winemakers, learn how well the chosen sites suit vine-growing, taste the excellent wines, and you may wonder why there isn't more movement outwards.

Rodington Vineyard, near Telford, Shropshire: an unusual family heritage

This is probably the most unusual of all the commercial vineyards included here. Rodington is the Midlands expression of a Punjabi farming heritage and was established in 2009 by Ram Dass Chahal, his wife Nirmala Devi, their daughters Manjit and Karin and sons Jai and Sagreev.

In the Punjab, Ram Dass Chahal grew up on the family farm, producing beet, corn and animal food. In England, his vegetable plot – a welcome relaxation from work in a Black Country foundry – soon overwhelmed the family's back garden. Next came an allotment. Then, as a retirement project, he bought a plot of land on the edge of Telford intending to plant

Rodington Vineyard and the blue tractor that features on the wine labels. RODINGTON VINEYARD

an apple orchard. Close by to the south lies the Wrekin; on the western horizon rise the foothills of the Welsh mountains. Nirmala Devi takes credit for the change of plan from apples to vines. By chance, she read a newspaper article on the increasing interest in English wine: 'I gave him the idea,' she proudly told BBC Radio 4 *On Your Farm* reporter Sybil Ruscoe in autumn 2016 as the last of the year's grapes were harvested.

Expert advice was sought, the sandy soil was deemed perfect for vines and planting began, with the 4 hectares becoming home to solaris, ortega, bacchus, seyval blanc, rondo and pinot noir, the red varieties cropping particularly well. It is very much a family enterprise, with the younger generation juggling full-time jobs with the demands of pruning, picking and other essential viticultural tasks. Family and friends join in for the harvest, which often carries on into the night. 'We're out with our mobile phones and torches,' Manjit Chahal told the radio interviewer. 'We've even thought of miners' helmets.'

'I wanted to plant something people could come round and enjoy,' Ram Dass Chahal added. But beyond giving pleasure through year-round opening, Rodington has been developed as a serious vineyard project. The family advanced cautiously, making sure initial plantings would flourish before adding more. The grapes are picked at optimum ripeness and the wine is made at Halfpenny Green Vineyard, forty minutes' drive to the south-east, where founder Martin Vickers and winemaker son Charles carry out contract winemaking for more than thirty vineyards as well as processing their own crop. (Halfpenny Green's own wines carried off five medals in the 2017 International Wine Challenge.) The Chahals' grapes, winery manager Ben Hunt told Ruscoe, consistently come in at above-average quality.

The wines are quality products too. Highlight of the numerous awards they have received was a silver medal in the 2016 International Wine Challenge for the Solaris Dry 2014. The judges loved its intense aromas and 'lively juicy green and red apple flavour'. But however far the project progresses, the Chahals won't forget its beginnings. The name on the wines is Blue Tractor, and the label shows that venerable, essential piece of agricultural equipment, the first they could afford when they bought the Rodington site.

Nutbourne Vineyards, near Pulborough, West Sussex: also keeping it in the family

One lasting memory I have from a calvados discovery tour in France is of a masterful father ensuring each of his sons followed a profession that was valuable in maintaining the family cider and calvados business. One was an accountant, to do the books; a second was a farmer, to ensure there were sheep to graze beneath the apple trees; a third made wardrobes from worn-out calvados barrels, which gave a wonderful scent to the clothes stored within. Nutbourne reminded me of that.

Peter Gladwin, who owns the vineyard with his wife Bridget, is a high-level special events caterer, with royal happenings and prestige locations featuring on his company CV. Two of his sons have followed him into cooking and serving food, running their own restaurants, and the third is a farmer. So, Nutbourne wine is important on the catering company and restaurant lists, and the restaurateurs serve meat from their brother's farm as well as foraging for other ingredients in the hedgerows around the vineyard. The bulk of the wine reaches consumers through these family businesses, with the rest bought by visitors to the vineyard or sold locally to other restaurants and hotels.

Here again, as in so many of the UK's vineyards, visitors are warmly welcomed, simply to walk through the vines or picnic, to join a formal tour or tutored tasting, or to arrange a corporate dinner or wedding reception in an evocative location. A former windmill with a balcony overlooking the vines, a purpose-built wine lodge and a smart marquee are the focus for all these, but the family emphasize that Nutbourne is a working farm and 'bigger on atmosphere than frills'.

Owning a vineyard hadn't been on the agenda for Peter and Bridget Gladwin. In 1991 they found the house they wanted – and it happened to come with already-planted vines, mostly such germanic varieties

Viewing spots over the vines: a rustic platform, a former windmill. NUTBOURNE VINEYARDS

as huxelrebe, reichensteiner and bacchus. Those remain the main components of their best-selling wine, the aromatic Sussex Reserve, a 'field blend' determined by the vineyard's crop each year and the first English still wine to win a gold medal in the International Wine & Spirit Competition. Some of the vines are well over thirty years old, but continue to produce good-quality grapes, if in small quantity, and the Gladwins like the style of wine from them.

Under the couple's stewardship, vineyard area has expanded to 10 hectares and the original varieties have been joined by a little pinot blanc and rather more pinot noir and chardonnay. Those two, plus reichensteiner, make the pink-tinged sparkling Nutty Brut. It's intriguing, says Bridget Gladwin, that this excellent-value bubbly can, in the same competition, carry off a gold medal alongside a bottle that costs at least half as much again. 'There are so many sparkling wines out there.' Since 2010 the Nutbourne wines have been made at the small on-site winery, where stainless steel modernity rubs shoulders with such classics as an eighty-year-old dosage machine. The winery is presided over by Owen Elias, ensuring not only quality but also character in the wines.

Three Choirs Vineyards, Newent, Gloucestershire: on to the next generation, of vines as well as people

Rare is the situation in the UK that vines need to be replaced because they're simply too old to be sensibly productive any more. At plenty of vineyards there has been replanting because of a change in the fashions for flavour or style of wine, but at Three Choirs there is an issue of age. The first vines were planted in 1973, and for once in those pioneering times the initiator was someone with experience of wine – Alan McKechnie, a local wine retailer who owned a fruit farm where grapes were to prove as happy as apples. From early on, his farm manager, Tom Day, was enthusiastic in developing the project. There is a human, as well as plant, generational story here: Day's son Simon, after time at Three Choirs, has branched out to become a respected consultant and winemaker in his own right,

and son-in-law Martin Fowke celebrated thirty years as the Three Choirs winemaker in 2018.

From the one-fifth of a hectare beginning to the present 30 hectares, the familiar germanic grape varieties have been the most important, and won't vanish yet: 'We have to keep our style, which is very popular,' said winery manager Kevin Shayle as he poured samples at the EWP 2017 tasting. 'We have to get the right balance between that and moving with the times.' Part of that 'right balance' has seen a change in emphasis from volume to 'producing the very best wines possible', as more and more Three Choirs bottles are sold locally rather than through the big supermarkets. The time when anything English was considered inferior is long gone, Shayle notes; now it is concern over the distances consumables travel and enthusiasm for local products that are proving to be major factors for buyers. He is delighted, too, that The Wine Society selected a classic Three Choirs blend as the first English wine to bear

At Three Choirs' Gloucestershire vineyard germanic varieties remain paramount. THREE CHOIRS VINEYARDS

Late-season work at Three Choirs' Hampshire vineyard. THREE CHOIRS VINEYARDS

its 'Society' own-brand label. 'That is a real stamp of approval.' Shayle is another experienced voice in the industry to predict that still wines could regain popularity and move up to equal the sparkling quantity.

With a long practice of welcoming visitors at the main Newent site, an emphasis on function activities at 2014-purchased Wickham Vineyard in Hampshire, and a selection of wines that range through fizz and blended or single-variety whites to oak-aged red, Three Choirs well understands the way to entice more wine drinkers to pour English into their glasses.

Sixteen Ridges, Shrawley, Worcestershire: where a reluctant farmer finally made the right decision

As a site description, the name just about says it all: Sixteen Ridges was an ancient arable field, the ridge and furrow pattern still clearly visible. But before the vines could be planted, a herd of cows had to relinquish their favourite pasture. Farmer John Ballard had sought the advice of consultant Simon Day about turning some

of his land into a vineyard – and that one field, Day told him, was by far the best place. For a good while, Ballard wouldn't countenance moving his cows, but in 2007 he was finally persuaded to allow vines onto the 2.4-hectare bowl-shaped field looking southwards down to the Severn Valley. Sandy loam topsoil lies above old Devonian sandstone, so drainage is good. Fruit ripens well, there is a sensible yield and the site was frost-free even in 2017, when clouds over Worcestershire gave welcome protection as so much of England's wine lands

Simon Day: enthusiastic about the potential of Herefordshire and Worcestershire. DUNCAN LOUGHREY/SIXTEEN RIDGES

froze. Pinot noir and seyval blanc grapes go into white and pink sparkling wines and still rosés, but the wine that has attracted most attention is the Early Red, from pinot noir précoce, an earlier-ripening relative of classic pinot noir.

Sixteen Ridges is far from Day's only interest, however. The vineyard project has expanded to include a second site, Redbank, near Ledbury in Herefordshire, where the soil above the sandstone is much more clayey and colder, though richer in nutrition for the vines. Once established, they do really well, and Day is delighted with the quick development of the bacchus planted there. Pinot noir and pinot noir précoce have followed. The winery built at Redbank makes the wine for both sites.

On a wider scale, when we talked in 2017 Day was optimistic for the wine future of Herefordshire and Worcestershire. Vineyard size would increase, as more would-be producers identified the potential of the area. 'We have everything that Kent has but a little bit better,' he emphasized, citing the success of asparagus crops (he could, perhaps, have expanded his comparison to include the Loire Valley, where vines are even more abundant than the stalky delight). The up-and-down topography is vine-friendly, frost is unusual, and, although there may not be the peak summer temperatures of some southern English locations, overall the climate is good by UK standards.

Despite his parents' insistence that he should get a 'proper job', Day couldn't resist a wine career route, which has taken him as far afield as Brown Brothers in Australia as well as to La Mare in Jersey and Denbies and Lamberhurst in England. Then, when his father retired from the Three Choirs, 'I came back to carry on what he had started.' But he had further ambitions, which in addition to the vineyards have taken him into consultancy, vine supply and contract winemaking, within the umbrella company Haygrove Evolution. A lot of English wines reflect his skill.

a'Beckett's Vineyard, near Devizes, Wiltshire: small is big in the west

Paul and Lynn Langham's vineyard proudly proclaims its position as Wiltshire's largest – but at barely 4 hectares that is tiny by standards further south-east. Still, from small beginnings great things grow, so who knows what the future holds for vines in this part of Wessex? The geology is excellent, greensand over chalk, similar to Ridgeview and Nyetimber, says Paul Langham, and he argues that there is less variability of weather here, further away from the sea. Over the years since 2001, when the couple planted their first vines, growing season temperatures have risen and that makes chardonnay a more realistic inclusion in the vineyard.

a'Beckett's offers plenty of variety for its size: its vine list is pinot noir (more than half the total), chardonnay, auxerrois, reichensteiner and seyval blanc. The auxerrois has thrived and provides an appealing point of difference. It is used both for a still wine and a sparkler, the latter named after Lynn's carpenter father Victor, who, despite not drinking alcohol himself, has supported the vineyard venture by helping to build the winery and joining the picking team. The still auxerrois was the first a'Beckett's wine I encountered, and I was impressed. Overall, still wine is the emphasis, in 2017 accounting for around 70 per cent of production, but demand more than personal choice is the prevailing influence.

Winbirri Vineyards, on the edge of the Norfolk Broads National Park: East Anglia gives the south coast a run for its money

'East Anglia is the best place in Britain for bacchus,' says Lee Dyer and he has justified his belief by winning awards for his own wine (*see* Chapter 4). The variety is 'the jewel in the crown' of a region that has huge potential for still wines in particular, he continues – there is more sun and less rain, especially as the grapes ripen. 'The flavour profiles and aromas we can achieve here from our vines are second to none.'

The vineyard, 10 hectares and expanding, was established in 2007 by Lee's fruit-farmer father Stephen. Lee took charge three years later, his previous lack of wine experience countered by intensive courses at Plumpton College, and commercial-scale plantings began, though Winbirri remains a family operation. Soil is light sandy loam above clay and the four vine sites were chosen to avoid frost pockets. In the very modern winery, fermentation temperatures are controlled by computer and maximum effort made to avoid oxidation and minimize use of sulphur dioxide, but Lee Dyer is insistent that what matters most is growing grapes of the highest quality. Alongside bacchus, the focus variety, there is pinot noir, solaris, rondo and seyval blanc. Unusually, more than one third of production is red wine, and that – from pinot noir especially – will remain important, alongside more sparkling wine. 'But,' said Dyer after the Decanter award, 'I'm certainly not jumping on the bandwagon and only heading in a sparkling route. The trophies we've won for our bacchus prove that our still wines can beat any English sparkling wine.'

Dyer emphasizes his long-term commitment to career and place, and to putting East Anglia more visibly on the UK vineyard map: 'I'm looking forward to giving Sussex, Kent and the rest of the south coast a good run for their money over the next few years.' That might prove a repeat of the past, for the Winbirri

Lee Dyer in the Winbirri vineyard. WINBIRRI VINEYARDS

name in Anglo-Saxon means 'wine grape' and there is plenty of evidence that the Saxons were active in and around the local village of Surlingham.

Giffords Hall Vineyard, near Long Melford, Suffolk: a different kind of employment

Linda Howard, another advocate of East Anglia's wine potential, admits she abandoned much of her business sense (she used to run an employment agency) when she first saw Giffords Hall: 'I fell in love with the place.' There were vines already, first planted in the 1980s by John Kemp on the sandy/clay soil of an ancient glacial river bed, but tending them was an entirely new experience for Linda and her husband Guy. 'We learned from the ground up.' Bacchus is among the vines that occupy just over 8 hectares of the Howards' land – hardly surprising, as more than half of all the bacchus grapes harvested in the UK come from East Anglia. But madeleine angevine is more important.

A fizz and a dry still wine are made from it, plus a pale, fresh and very appealing rosé where the colour is from the addition of a little rondo. The rosé comes in magnum as well as bottle, a summery treat that more still wine producers might copy. In many of its grape choices, Giffords Hall characterizes current practice: it also grows pinot noir and pinot blanc, two more of the varieties on the increase in the area. 'Our wines have a delicate floral character very typical of the region,' Linda Howard emphasizes.

Kemp, the vineyard's originator and renowned for being one of that rare UK breed, a winemaker who foot-trod his grapes, bowed out from his long vinous career reluctantly. He continued with a small area of vines after selling Giffords Hall in 2004 and finally retired only in 2011. Even then the grape connection wasn't over. He and his wife Jeanie commissioned a local architect to turn their redundant winery into a carbon-neutral home, and in 2016 it was declared greenest building in the Suffolk 'green Oscar' awards.

Ready to harvest at Albourne. ALBOURNE ESTATE

Albourne Estate, near Hurstpierpoint, East Sussex: a growing new career

In the UK wine industry there is understandable scepticism over some new entrants (as there was over plenty of their predecessors): people with no background in any kind of agriculture and no long-cherished ambition to make wine. Alison Nightingale is one of the newcomers firmly countering such doubts. She and her husband, Nick Cooper, chose their fleeing-from-London location simply as somewhere calm to bring up their children, and while he continued commuting she looked for a new career she could combine with family responsibilities. Wine, she decided, could be 'a more creative, fulfilling and balanced path'. Fast forward just over a decade (which included four years of part-time study at Plumpton College) and Nightingale was becoming

a name of note: from 2015 her Albourne Estate wines have carried off major awards and regularly sell out. Bacchus, ortega and pinots blanc, gris and noir go into still wines and the three champagne varieties are destined for fizz – the first, launched in summer 2017, a blanc de blancs.

Before wine, Nightingale's main career direction was in multi-national marketing, and that expertise shows in what are probably the most distinctively attractive of all English wine bottle labels, illustrating the wildlife around the estate – buzzard on the bacchus and green woodpecker on the Estate Selection blend are examples – the work of local artist Louise Body. Sustaining that wildlife is part of the estate philosophy, with solar panels and high levels of building insulation keeping energy use green and the non-vine areas maintained as grassland and hedgerows to high environmental stewardship standards.

Tinwood Estate, near Chichester, West Sussex: where vines replace vegetables

Tinwood Estate is another of the many vineyards in the far south of England where you can almost smell the sea, which here lies 9 kilometres to the south. This is one of the large new vineyards in Sussex, with a little over 25 hectares of chardonnay, pinot noir and pinot meunier planted from 2007 at the foot of the South Downs. Vines should feel at home here, as there is every likelihood that the Cistercian monks at neighbouring Boxgrove Priory had produced wine for their own consumption many centuries earlier. The soil is very vine-friendly, well-drained flinty loam above the layer of chalk that is starting to head down below the English Channel before its emergence in Champagne, and the location offers plenty of warm sunshine and little risk of frost.

What's unusual is the modern link with one of the pioneers of English sparkling wine, Ridgeview. In 2006 Mike Roberts, Ridgeview's founder, sold a 25 per cent

Lodges with a view of the Tinwood vines. AUTHOR

share in his business to the Dekker family, who had long grown vegetables and arable crops on the Tinwood land but, at the instigation of son Art, were moving into wine grapes. It suited both parties. The arrangement guaranteed the Roberts family a necessary additional supply of meticulously cared-for grapes as they increased the production of their signature sparkling wines; Art Dekker had no plans to build a winery but wanted to be able to sell wines with a Tinwood label, so having access to Ridgeview's winemaking facility was ideal.

While visitors do not have the chance to see how wine is made, there is plenty of alternative entertainment, with a variety of tours and events. Some visitors don't even need to drive home, for three purpose-built lodges, floor-to-ceiling windows overlooking the vines, are available to rent. Just a couple of kilometres or so from the vineyard lies one of Sussex's most popular attractions: Goodwood, historic home of the Dukes of Richmond and Gordon, with its racecourse, motor circuit and small aerodrome. Dekker told me of one lodge guest, in his seventies, who came to stay and fulfilled three of the items on a bucket list of wishes: flying in a Spitfire, driving a racing car and tasting English sparkling wine.

Painshill Park, Cobham, Surrey: eighteenth-century splendour restored

Charles Hamilton would surely be a happy man if he could return today to the elaborate landscape park he created in the mid-eighteenth century. Not only has the Painshill Park Trust – whose president is a Hamilton descendant – restored the elaborate planting, fanciful follies and sinuous lake, but there is more. The vineyard from which Charles Hamilton made wine 'with a finer flavour than the best champaign' has been re-created, and sparkling wine is again being made from its grapes. All that makes Painshill Park one of the most appealing places for a historically minded wine tourist to visit, bringing together the past and the present of Britain's wine story.

The vines now growing on the 1-hectare south-facing hill sloping down to the lake are pinot noir, chardonnay and seyval blanc, their grapes turned into a white and a pink fizz. Although Charles Hamilton made his wines on site, there is no winery now, so the grapes go off to Bluebell Vineyard Estates on the edge of Ashdown Forest in central Sussex, a specialist in sparkling wines since its establishment in 2005. The result comes back for sale in the park's shop, and proves that Charles Hamilton's choice of site still makes excellent sense more than 250 years on.

The restoration of Painshill Park is a remarkable story. First, a little history. The 34-year-old ninth son of the sixth Earl of Abercorn came to Painshill in 1738, inspired by two Grand Tours in Europe to create through 'living paintings' a style of garden then unknown in England. Charles Hamilton's aim was to move away from formality to something much wilder though still carefully designed. His plantings, notes the current Painshill Park Guide, 'were at the cutting edge of English landscape design' and with them, the new species he introduced and the classical follies he built, he 'changed the face of the English landscape forever'. Creating so elaborate an estate over three decades cost a huge amount of money and in 1773 Hamilton was obliged to sell, paying off his debts and moving away. The buyer, Benjamin Bond Hopkins, MP, an eccentric with a reputation for being tight with money despite his personal wealth, built himself an impressive new mansion and maintained the park, though his design ideas differed somewhat from those of Hamilton.

A succession of owners followed Bond Hopkins and by the 1970s little of the original grandeur survived. The park had been split up and the parts sold off, with the house converted into private homes. A group of concerned local residents, with the support of the Garden History Society and the Georgian Group, persuaded the local authority – Elmbridge Borough Council – to buy some 63 hectares of Hamilton's site, by then a Grade I listed landscape, before all traces of his dream vanished. The Painshill Park Trust was established, restoration began and the result is the delight today, the wine included.

Vines are back where Charles Hamilton planted them in the eighteenth century. AUTHOR

Sharpham Vineyard, near Totnes, Devon: battles past, history present

Sharpham is another place where eighteenth-century history is important, though the actual vineyard roots don't dip so deep into the past. The mansion that sits atop the estate's vine-clad slopes is the product, literally, of the capture of the richest prize of the Seven Years War. Captain Philemon Pownoll made a lot of money when he took the Spanish treasure ship *Ermiona* in 1762. With it, he bought the Sharpham estate on the banks of the River Dart and commissioned a fine Palladian villa to replace the existing Tudor house. Sadly, he was killed in action before he had a chance to enjoy the result. Skip on to the 1960s and ownership by the Ash

family, and the plan was to make cheese from the milk of their newly acquired herd of Jersey cows. No, scoffed the experts, no one will want it. Wrong – the cheese proved immensely popular and remains so, though the cows now graze on pastures a few kilometres away, close to the modern dairy that twenty-first-century health controls require.

With cheese, why not wine? Maurice Ash, who loved all things French, decided there must be vines. His initial few hundred square metres grew to 3.4 hectares, the vine variety increased, visitors on the themed retreats (from the mid-1980s Sharpham became a charitable trust promoting well-being and sustainable living) enjoyed the product, with Sharpham cheese, and the modern pattern was established. The oldest vines date

A splendidly scenic site for vines: Sharpham vineyard in a meander of the River Dart. SHARPHAM WINE AND CHEESE

from the 1980s and germanic varieties predominate, with madeleine angevine particularly happy in the rich red Devon sandstone soil on a site where frost is rare and the windbreak trees are sufficiently spaced to allow a breeze to stir away fungal problems. The choice of raw material is expanded by grapes from the 8.5-hectare Sandridge Barton vineyard across the Dart, bringing in bacchus, pinot noir, chardonnay and more madeleine angevine. With that broad palette, Sharpham offers fifteen different wines, 'so everyone will find at least one wine they like' said assistant winemaker Tommy Grimshaw, pouring them one after another into my glass.

As we walked the vineyard, that rich red soil added to the rainbow of mud my boots have collected over the years. Glass in hand, allowing me to sample the finished product beside the plants from which it came, Grimshaw introduced me to more of Sharpham's pre-wine history. Like the visitors who wander through the rows of vines dropping steeply down towards the river, we arrived at Philemon Pownoll Quay. This was the eighteenth-century unloading point for the ships bringing building materials for the new villa – including the Portland stone that was a gift to the captain from a grateful government. Sitting there on a sunny summer evening, with a refill in that glass, the river flowing past, perhaps a family of seals cavorting in the water – that's English wine bliss.

Certainly many wine tourists are tempted by what Sharpham offers. Some 10,000-plus visitors come each year, and buy half the estate's wine. Almost all of the rest is sold locally. 'The vast majority have never tried English wine before and lots of them come because they want to find out more,' explained Grimshaw.

The history lesson wasn't over, nor was the wine walk. Further along the riverbank the wreck of the SS *Kingswear* appears. Former ferry on the river, she was a hospital isolation ship in the First World War. Even at the end of her life not everything was left to rust away in those familiar waters, for the engine was removed and powers the current river ferry. Then a steep push up the hill, past the 1970s Lamborghini tractor that has been kept long beyond its deserved retirement date because it is small enough to fit between the rows, took

us to the reward of more wine to taste and a café serving food cooked over vine trimmings.

The most modern history at Sharpham lies in bottles. Its wine library is a comprehensive source of everything produced since 1996 and just occasionally there is a chance to try a venerable bottle. Grimshaw recalls the 2004 Estate Selection with enormous pleasure: 'It tasted extraordinary.' And from the old to the new: one of the four madeleine angevine wines made at Sharpham is Devon's answer to beaujolais nouveau, from vine to bottle in four weeks so that it can go on sale the same day as the French classic. It came about with true national spirit, as a small but pertinent retort to the French ban on UK beef in the time of BSE.

And on that very patriotic note, we'll end our tour.

Sharpham's vineyard dips down towards the River Dart. SHARPHAM WINE AND CHEESE

Chapter 10

Enjoying English Wine, and Being Part of It

IT'S ALL VERY WELL TO READ ABOUT ENGLISH WINE, but experiencing it will confirm the enjoyment it can give. Those who grow the vines and make the wine are well aware of that, and wine tourism is increasingly important in every area of the UK where wine is made. That tourism can, however, take very many different forms.

The most obvious is vineyard visits, and there is no better way to start, particularly as most visits end with a tasting. While many vineyards welcome visitors, the experiences they offer vary considerably. At the most basic, there will be footpaths through the vines, perhaps with a guiding map or a brief explanatory leaflet. Usually this will be free. Next step up is a guided tour, for which there is likely to be a charge. At a small operation the tour may be led by the owner or winemaker, at a larger one there will be someone whose role is solely to show visitors around. Some guided tours will be a simple extension of the walk-it-yourself visit; others will be much more comprehensive and also include the winery if wine is made on the spot. Some places may split the experience, with vineyard-only or winery-only tours. If you've never been to a winery before, seeing the amount of equipment involved in making wine will be a revelation. Remember, though, that during much of the year not a lot is actually happening in either vineyard or winery – most activity is at harvest and shortly afterwards. There are also times, harvest again and spraying, for example, when visitors' freedom to roam will be restricted.

One tour where the distance covered is particularly long (at Denbies Wine Estate in Surrey) takes the weight off visitors' feet by transporting them through the vineyard in a 'land-train' towed by a 4x4. Quite

Pointing the way round the vineyard, at Biddenden. AUTHOR

a few vineyards (Sharpham Vineyard in Devon and Furleigh Estate in Dorset are among them) equip tour participants with glasses in natty holders and pour wines

On-the-spot explanation of vine planting, by Charles Simpson.
SIMPSONS WINE ESTATE

the tour – cheese or charcuterie platters are popular. Prices vary, but they are usually in line with the extent of the experience, perhaps £8–£15 for a simple guided tour with two or three wines to sample, around £25 for a tour with tasting of more wines accompanied by something to nibble, more for a sophisticated meal with partnering wine. Just occasionally, those on a tour will be invited to take home all the bottles opened for them to taste.

Lots of vineyards are happy to see children as well as adults, though obviously under-18s can't join in tastings. Interactive trails, with animals or other items to spot along the way and perhaps the prospect of a prize at the finish, are a way of entertaining youngsters (Bolney Wine Estate in West Sussex is one offering this).

After a tour, plenty of vineyards provide places to sit and relax with a glass in hand, looking out over the vines. One of the loveliest is Camel Valley in Cornwall, where visitors can buy the wines in smaller or larger measures

alongside the very vines from which they came. Many offer group visits, from wine club outings to school excursions, from hen parties to open-air services among the vines (a'Beckett's Vineyard in Wiltshire has been the location for several of the last of these). Plenty provide food alongside the wine at the tasting that ends

Members of the Albury wine club on a vineyard tour. ALBURY ORGANIC VINEYARD

Sipping in the sun, on Camel Valley's terrace.

CAMEL VALLEY WINES

to extend the tasting experience while enjoying the view over the vines and the Camel River valley beyond. That reminds me of a (true) story set not in England but in France. An English couple with minimal knowledge of French fancied an afternoon glass of wine, saw tables and bottles set out close to the roadside and a sign saying '*Dégustation*'. An outdoor wine bar, they thought, stopped, sat and started to sip. They were puzzled, though, at the rather small quantities in their glasses, and beckoned the owner over, indicating they'd like a top-up. He, also somewhat puzzled, obliged. Two or three glasses of the same wine later, they asked for the bill – only to learn, through much gesticulating, that this was a free sampling of the adjoining vineyard's product. Very red-faced, they finally understood what *dégustation*

meant, and felt obliged to buy a case of bottles to make up for their gaffe. Somehow, I don't think French tourists in England would make the same mistake (an increasing number do turn up at wineries in perfidious Albion and appreciate the tasting experience).

But back to the English enjoyment theme. The experience can go much further than tours and simple tastings. The 'Be a Winemaker' evenings at Hambledon Vineyard in Hampshire are hugely popular. Host is the effusive and knowledgeable Joe Wadsack, who leads participants through the sparkling wine process, lets them taste the results of different dosage and then encourages them to blend their own cuvée – and at the end they take home a bottle of 'their' wine. Also deservedly much in demand is the 'young wine' tasting

evening run by Greyfriars in its newly dug chalk cave just off the A3 in Surrey. Here the samples are base wines and blends from the new vintage, to compare with the wines currently on sale – a glimpse into the future expanded by the inclusion of other finished but not yet released wines. These are examples of 2017 initiatives, but could well continue, and further imaginative combinations of entertainment and education are included in English Wine Week and local wine festivals.

Opportunities abound to get more involved in the wine-producing process. Lots of vineyards offer 'adopt a vine' schemes, with Chapel Down and Three Choirs among the pioneers. The annual fee will normally include the allocation of some bottles, or discounts on purchases of the vineyard's wine, and an invitation to visit. Usually, the vines available are already planted, but not at the new Mannings Heath vineyard in West Sussex in April 2017. It wasn't the normal interested public who were involved, but wine writers. We rarely have the chance to get our hands dirty, so perhaps that's why there was such enthusiasm for planting the baby pinot meunier vines, each with a label bearing the planter's name. They were among the million new vines that went into UK ground in 2017. Like the majority of the grapes to come from the biggest-ever planting in these islands' vine history, their fruit is intended for sparkling wine, so I must wait until 2023 to taste the

wine to which 'my' vine has contributed. Whether the design of golf trollies – or buggies, given the extent of the Mannings Heath courses – will have to evolve to include a place for glasses and a cool box to hold the bottle of fizz remains to be seen. The entrepreneurial owner Penny Streeter will almost certainly have thought of that already, and I have no doubt she is planning further schemes to involve the wine-enthusiastic public in the estate.

At plenty of vineyards extra hands are needed at harvest time. Just occasionally this is a formal, paid-for experience, but more often help in gathering in the grapes is welcomed from friends, family, local people or those from further away. Nutbourne Vineyard in Sussex has displayed its appeal for volunteer pickers in the village post office, while Brightwell Vineyard close to the Thames in Oxfordshire has tempted volunteer pickers by rewarding their four-hour morning effort with lunch – accompanied by Brightwell wine – and a chance afterwards to watch the grape processing. Be warned: picking is hard work and you end up very sticky indeed.

Rare are the producers who offer hands-on action in the winery itself. One notable exception is London Cru (Roberson Wine), the 'city winery', housed in a former gin distillery close to Earls Court exhibition centre and equipped with the full panoply of winemaking equipment, from presses to oak barrels. Winemaking

Sorting newly arrived bacchus grapes at London Cru. LONDON CRU

there began with grapes transported in from France and Italy, joined from 2014 with fruit from English vineyards. Paid-for 'winemaker for a day' sessions are regularly on offer.

Volunteers are also invited to work alongside staff at busy times, helping with sorting and pressing grapes and at the bottling and labelling stages. Winemaker for five years Gavin Monery, an Australian whose impressive vinous CV includes spells at a legendary biodynamic vineyard in his homeland's Margaret River region as well as in Burgundy and the Rhône Valley, reasoned: 'We hope that the opportunity to get involved with the winemaking process, to touch, see and taste the product from grape through to the finished bottle will inspire people to care that little bit more about wine and how they choose to enjoy it.'

There is another way of feeling immersed in wine production (not literally, of course, for health and safety rules are tough enough without a Duke of Clarence experience being offered), and that is to stay on a vineyard. Purpose-built self-catering lodges with views over the vines are a popular choice – the three at Tinwood Estate in West Sussex are aptly named 'Chardonnay', 'Pinot Noir' and 'Pinot Meunier'. Other accommodation possibilities include converted barns, comfortable cottages, B&B rooms, boutique hotels, camping and caravan sites, even shepherds' huts, though perhaps the most romantic is a converted Georgian bathing house with the River Dart flowing by only metres away, on Sharpham Estate, Devon. Talking of romance, lots of vineyards put themselves forward as wedding venues,

and there must be something special about toasting the happy couple with fizz made from the vines outside the window.

Music and wine are perfect partners, and a number of vineyards host opera performances. Breaky Bottom in East Sussex was one truly atmospheric location, and the experience has been enjoyed at others including Albury in Surrey, Court Garden in East Sussex and Three Choirs in Gloucestershire. Elsewhere, there can be art alongside the vines – High Clandon Estate in Surrey has made a speciality of this.

You can, of course, also enjoy home vinous produce at plenty of events at non-wine locations. For example, in 2017 Coates & Seely became exclusive sparkling wine partner for Goodwood Racecourse, Chapel Down began a four-year sponsorship of the Oxford & Cambridge Boat Race and Nyetimber continued its involvement with the Cowes Week sailing event.

Back in the vineyards, one essential date each year for welcoming happenings is English Wine Week, coinciding with the late spring bank holiday. It has grown and grown, spreading beyond the places where vines grow to involve restaurants and bars and wine retailers, and the events become more imaginative every year. They are a great way to learn and enjoy, and good places to buy bottles to take home.

On the subject of buying, year round, plenty of vineyards run wine clubs whose members receive discounts on wine plus other benefits in return for a

Appropriately named lodge on the Tinwood estate. AUTHOR

A place to stay, nestled among the vines at Three Choirs' Gloucestershire vineyard. THREE CHOIRS VINEYARDS

subscription fee. They can be well worthwhile if you like a particular place's products. Otherwise, English wines are increasingly readily available in supermarkets and wine merchants, large and small, and there are walk-in or online sellers whose entire stock comes from within the UK.

Among such specialists, the first to be established was the English Wine Centre, at Alfriston in East Sussex, set up in 1972 by Christopher Ann. A well-remembered figure in the revival of the home product, Ann was prominent in industry organizations and ran the English Wine Festival for 21 years. The centre became known for its tastings, museum, restaurant and as wedding location, as well as for its impressive choice of bottles. When Ann retired after thirty-five years, Christine and Colin Munday took over and continued the devel-

opment of a remarkable resource, surely offering the widest choice of English wines in any single place. Their time in charge has seen amazing changes, Christine Munday told me: 'Ten years ago there was only one good red wine and hardly any sparkling wine – it felt like a teenage industry. Now it is in its early twenties.' Customers' confidence in English wine has soared, and only once has there been a complaint that the English Wine Centre offered no bottles from beyond Britain.

The very much newer Exceptional English Wine Company has shown how challenging it is to run a shop devoted solely to English wine. This venture was founded in 2014 by Iain Heggie and Carolyn and Robin Butler, at the Cowdray Park polo ground site at Midhurst in West Sussex. Part of the aim was to find out for themselves who made the best and most popular

Iain Heggie: a personal way to spread the word. AUTHOR

Wine in its proper place, on the table

England's wines, bubbly or light still whites, make great aperitifs, but much of the pleasure of wine is in partnership with food. Who better to recommend pairings than the people who are responsible for what's in the bottles? I asked a number of them, and their suggestions follow. There was one word – 'delicious!' – that was used very frequently to describe their chosen matches. 'Amazing!' appeared too, and for both the exclamation mark was always there.

Let one very experienced palate, that of Kevin Sutherland, winemaker at Bluebell Vineyard Estates, briefly explain the theory behind the pleasure: 'The key to food and wine matching is to assess the basic components of each and then find a balance between those components so that they don't overpower each other.' On sparkling wines specifically, he argues that it is wrong to think that they can be enjoyed only as an aperitif – they can also be excellent with many dishes, especially fish. 'In general, the acidity of sparkling wines makes them great for matching with slightly fatty or sweet foods, as the acidity cuts through in the way a lemon can cut through and cleanse the palate when eating smoked salmon.'

His own recommended combination? Bluebell's Hindleap Late-Disgorged Blanc de Blancs 2008 with 'something really indulgent like oysters or lobster'. His reasoning: 'The extra ageing the wine has had (seven years in the cellar), provides depth and complexity while the bubbles provide the perfect textural contrast to the smooth velvety texture of oysters or the richness of lobster. This 2008 wine is underpinned by the characteristic freshness of chardonnay with lots of lemon- and lime-zest notes that go toe to toe with butter or cream sauces.'

English wines – the Butlers were planting vines close by at Trotton and needed to choose where to have their wines made. But they also wanted to spread the word about how good English wine has become and what excellent value for money the fizz often is compared to many champagnes. Still wine proves a harder sell, Heggie has found, with too many of the UK wine-buying public reluctant to dig deep enough into their pockets to buy it. In summer 2017 he made the decision to add some non-UK still wines to the selection.

Heggie told me, however, of a particular feature of the business that he hoped would mean the Exceptional English Wine Company could continue as a retail outlet for much of the UK's top fizz. He has developed a personalized corporate gifting service offering major UK companies tastings of English sparkling wines and sending their choices, with well-presented information, tasting notes and individual messages, to clients or others they wished to thank. The initiative snowballed, providing effective publicity for English wine as well as being an astute business move. Keeping the Midhurst base will help spread that publicity, through tastings in the shop, at other locations and at customers' homes, where pre-dinner appetiser sessions have proved popular.

Which conveniently leads on to drinking rather than simply tasting.

Plenty more of the winemakers I approached favoured the fishy theme. Kristin Syltevik, of Oxney Organic Estate, went back to her Norwegian heritage to recommend Oxney Classic sparkling wine with a Scandinavian-inspired seafood smorgasbord of smoked salmon, freshly caught and cooked prawns, sweet-and-sour cucumber salad, potato salad and thin

slices of rye bread. Her choice, she emphasized, 'is a great food wine, not just a special occasions 'drink with nibbles'.

For Nick Wenman and daughter Lucy Letley, the perfect partner for their Albury Estate Blanc de Blancs has to be smoked trout and watercress tart served with a lemon crème fraîche dressing. The fish would come from Tillingbourne Trout Farm and the watercress from the spring-fed beds at Kingfishers farm shop, both close to the Surrey vineyard and two of 'lots of great food producers on our doorstep'. 'Wines with high acidity are a good match for high-acidity foods, and the lemon crème fraîche complements the wine perfectly,' adds Letley.

Gavin Monery at London Cru is another to favour fish: salmon and avocado poke, his take on a Hawaiian classic. The two main ingredients spend time in a marinade of red and green onions, soy sauce, sugar, ground ginger, sesame oil and sesame seeds, then are served on cooled steamed white rice. Baker Street bacchus is

the perfect accompaniment: 'The acid cuts through the fat and matches the flavours well.'

Nicholas Coates spoke of the inspired matching of the delicate citrus and white fruits of Coates & Seely Blanc de Blancs La Perfide 2009 with cod in a shellfish sauce served with celeriac purée. That was one of the dishes on a 'thrilling' tasting menu put together by Christophe Marleix, executive chef at the Dorchester Grill, and Vincent Pastorello, the Dorchester's head of wine.

Red wine, too, can work with fish, as Simon Day, winemaker at Sixteen Ridges Estate, discovered with a panic-prompted choice. 'I unexpectedly found this combination at a last-minute family dinner party,' he explains. 'I pulled a bottle of our Pinot Noir 2014 from the rack, slightly too cool, but opened and poured immediately. The dish was Jamie Oliver's salmon en croûte with watercress and spinach. The aromas of violet, dried cherry and raspberry, following on with the gentle earthy tannin structure of the wine, were the

perfect match to the rich salmon, with earthy, peppery flavours from the spinach and watercress. Everyone loved it!'

Simpler than all these is the message from Linda Howard, of Giffords Hall Vineyard: that madeleine angevine is 'the' wine to have with mussels.

But there are plenty of possibilities beyond fish, and the wine doesn't always need to bubble. Corinne Seely, head winemaker at Exton Park in Hampshire, remembers the 'amazing' pairing of the estate's sparkling Pinot Meunier Rosé with wild mushroom tortellini, wilted spinach and cep cream sauce at a gourmet dinner cooked by Aimée Reddick at Luton Hoo. 'The saltiness and strength of the mushrooms perfectly balanced the floral side and the spices of the meunier.'

Cherie Spriggs, head winemaker at Nyetimber, agrees that sparkling wines are not just about pairing with canapés and seafood. She suggested Nyetimber Rosé with a more textured dish, roasted guinea fowl with a salad of watercress, butternut, pine nuts and parmesan.

Moving on to still wines with meaty main courses, let's tour the world. Mike and Hilary Wagstaff at Greyfriars Vineyard know the match for what might be Britain's favourite dish, chicken tikka masala: 'Our aromatic pinot gris really hits the spot with spicy food, especially Indian. The acid in the wine tones down the heat and leaves room for the fruitiness to express itself.'

While on an Asian theme, Martin Fowke and Kevin Shayle, respectively head winemaker and winery manager at Three Choirs Vineyard, point to Estate Reserve Siegerrebe as a great choice with Thai food, which enhances the lychee and rose-petal characteristics of the rich, aromatic wine. Closer to home, Howard Corney of Court Garden Vineyard recommends his Ditchling Rosé, from rondo and dornfelder grapes, with salade niçoise or paella. And for Paul Langham of a'Becketts Vineyard the perfect pairing for the estate's pinot noir is English roast lamb, garlic, rosemary and 'all the trimmings'.

As the meal draws to a close, there are more choices. The Wagstaffs suggest Greyfriars Blanc de Blancs with rhubarb and custard, while Emma Rice, winemaker at Hattingley Valley, believes the estate's peach and elderflower-scented Entice dessert wine can be enjoyed with any pudding, as well as being excellent with English

Destined for a dinner with English pinot noir? No, these sheep are part of a Nyetimber vineyard project. NYETIMBER

A match made in
Devon heaven:
Sharpham cheese
and Sharpham
wine. SHARPHAM WINE
AND CHEESE

blue cheese. The wines from Sharpham Vineyard also work well with cheese – especially that produced from the milk of the estate's herd of Jersey cows.

Restaurant chefs, both at the top, internationally renowned level and at the many excellent small but very serious UK restaurants showcasing local ingredients, are increasingly enthusiastic about linking English food and wine, so here are just two appetisers.

From the Parsons Table in Arundel, West Sussex, Liz (front of house) and Lee (chef) Parsons recommend Nutty Brut sparkling wine from Nutbourne Vineyards, a regular on their list, with one of Lee's fishy starters, olive oil poached sea trout with soused beetroot, samphire and chive crème fraîche. The match works particularly well, they say, for lots of reasons: the crispness of the wine cuts the richness of the fish and adds balance, the earthy undertones of the sweet beetroots are enhanced by the vibrancy and acidity of the wine, the crème fraîche adds another layer of flavour and texture that promotes the fruity notes of the wine.

A starter match is also suggested by Brett Woonton and Charlie Young, whose Vinoteca wine bars in London have more than a dozen English wines on their list. A particularly successful seasonal combination, they say, is poached white English asparagus, egg, vinaigrette and hazelnuts with aromatic Camel Valley Bacchus.

Main meals apart, there are other times when English wines can be enjoyed, even early in the morning. The most imaginative wine pairing of all comes from Liam Idzikowski, who reckons it is hard to beat his Lyme Bay Blanc de Noirs fizz with an Ulster fry-up. That is, he explains, 'a full English breakfast, with three extra slices of fried bread'. 'If there are mushrooms, it's even better,' he adds.

Later in the day, why not a glass of sparkling rosé with a cream tea? The berry flavours in the wine go well with those in the jam on the scones and again the acidity cuts through the cream's richness. Or for true summer fun, try the recipe for 'Frosé' from Bolney Wine Estate. Combine frozen cubes of Bolney Rosé with a little grenadine syrup in a blender, pour the 'slushie' result into pretty glasses and garnish with strawberries. Don't overdo the syrup, say Bolney's Sam and Charlotte Linter: 'We want to keep things fresh and dry like the wine itself.'

Fine with a fishy starter.
NUTBOURNE VINEYARDS

Chapter 11

WHAT DOES THE FUTURE HOLD?

THE LAST WEEK OF APRIL 2017 WAS A TIME OF lows and highs for English wine. In the early hours of Wednesday the first of a succession of 'worst in a generation' frosts struck vineyards in Hampshire. It was particularly unwelcome as the vine buds had burst open a fortnight ahead of their normal time and the young leaves were unusually well developed. At affected vineyards the year's potential crop was halved. In the middle of the same day, a viticulturist in Sussex was asked what future precautions he would take against frost affecting the 38,000 vines he was currently planting. 'None should be necessary,' came the emphatic reply.

Of course there are differences between the Hampshire sites worst hit that day, such as the comparatively exposed Leckford Estate vineyard close to Stockbridge, and the new Mannings Heath vineyard on the outskirts of Horsham in Sussex, with its ring of protective woodland. But those two experiences can serve as a valuable example of both the predicaments and the optimism within a still-new industry. What will the future hold? Will the UK's erratic climate continue

Hoar frost on a vine tendril. VIV BLAKEY/RATHFINNY WINE ESTATE

Healthy young leaves on a Painshill vine in April 2017 – frost was to strike the next night. AUTHOR

to set so many traps that wine grape-growing will never be much more than a marginal occupation? Or will the increasing knowledge and skill of viticulturists and winemakers, aided by a warmer growing season, build on the progress of the last few decades so that producing wine becomes a reliable, mainstream business?

Later that April Wednesday, Becky Hull, the buyer responsible for the largest selection of English wine stocked by any supermarket, confirmed to me that one of the biggest challenges she and others selling in quantity faced was the unreliability of supply, vintage on vintage. Ominously, a hailstorm was pounding the Waitrose head office on a Berkshire industrial estate, hardly wine land itself but with vineyards not far away. I'd just driven the 30 kilometres from the replanted historic vineyard at Painshill Park in Surrey, where the well-opened vine buds had been basking in warm sunshine, with no hint of frost damage. Those contrasts were further reminders of risk and hope.

To return to the matter of making available to mainstream drinkers the wine produced in the UK, and specifically how Waitrose, as a major supermarket, handles that. At the time we talked, Becky Hull had built the company list to around one hundred choices: some on the shelves in a broad raft of stores, more sold only in branches close to the individual vineyards, but all available online. That impressive expression of support began soon after the earliest 'better-than-champagne' acclaim and, over Christmas 2016, had reached a level at which one bottle of English sparkling wine was bought by Waitrose customers alongside every ten bottles of champagne they selected.

That might not sound a lot, until you read another statistic: in that year, the home-grown product comprised less than 1 per cent of all wine sold in England. So, nearly 10 per cent of sales at the prestige end of the fizz market is important. Hull revealed further significant information on customers' buying habits, relating to product loyalty and what they choose as alternatives: when they have bought a particular bottle of English sparkling wine, they might not always go for the same one again, but they will buy another English fizz.

This shows the affection – of Waitrose customers at least – for the home product, especially when it has bubbles, and the overall rise in sales confirms that wine-knowledgeable customers who are prepared to try English wine enjoy it and keep on buying it. But there could be much more opportunity to grow the market if a bigger base of English still wine was available. 'People buy into a country,' Hull explained, 'then on special occasions they will buy a bottle of fizz from that country. We don't have that base with English wine, so it's holding back sparkling wine.' Much as Hull would like to broaden the Waitrose choice of English still wines, there is a way to go before they consistently match the quality of the fizz, she believes. In her view, it would help both consumers and retailers if there were a new standard to distinguish those of a higher level. More retailers taking English still wine seriously would be another step forward, as would a higher available volume, which could bring production costs down and perhaps be reflected in prices – persuading consumers to try English wine when Chilean or South African or Spanish is half the price is an uphill struggle.

In an expression of growing confidence in consumer interest, in autumn 2017 highly regarded direct seller The Wine Society put its own label on an English still wine for the first time (its Exhibition English sparkling wine, made by Ridgeview, had by then been on sale for more than three years). The still white choice was a blend from Three Choirs Vineyards in Gloucestershire, whose wines The Society had already offered for several years. The sub-£10 price was unusual for an English wine – a price, buyer Freddy Bulmer told me, largely due to the fact that Three Choirs is a long-established and commercially oriented operation, where many of the initial costs have been absorbed.

It is difficult, he believes, for UK wine producers to sell at low prices. For most there aren't the economies of

Vines at Three Choirs' Gloucestershire vineyard, source of supply to The Wine Society. THREE CHOIRS VINEYARDS

scale seen in many other wine countries. Initial expenses in particular are high and need to be recouped, there is much costly attention to detail in vineyard and winery, and of course yields are low. And then there is the further hurdle of introducing drinkers to grape varieties they have never heard of before. Convincing consumers that the wines are value for money can be hard work, but Bulmer is certain that knowledge and understanding will grow. 'It's fascinating to be here, in an industry in relative infancy. Watching it grow is exciting.'

Back on the high street, Marks & Spencer has been significantly increasing its range of both still and sparkling English wine, and early in 2017 reported 'phenomenal growth', though within a very small overall base. It too has taken a supportive role, sponsoring a final-year student at Plumpton College, who makes a wine for the company – student number four's wine, vintage 2016, was a still white from the three champagne varieties. The first M&S scholarship student, Collette O'Leary, who moved on to become wine development manager at Bluebell Vineyard Estates, was responsible, with another Plumpton alumnus, for a single-vineyard bacchus that joined the supermarket's regional range in 2017.

M&S English wine buyer Elizabeth Kelly has been happy with the increasing quality and range of wines available, but less content that 'there aren't enough grapes to go round', putting pressure on prices. But for whites and rosés, particularly pinot noir rosés, she believes many buyers – especially in London and similarly wine-savvy locations – are prepared to pay a premium. Better consumer understanding of English wine is crucial, and 'the message seems to be getting out there'. She has contributed on a personal scale: 'I've converted most of my friends now!' Such individual effort should not to be underestimated, for word of mouth is a powerful promotion tool.

Buyers of English wine fall into a 'very specific demographic', says organic grower Kristin Syltevik, whose previous expertise before she founded Oxney Estate was in public relations. They are young professionals who are yet to start a family and well-off older people, groups ready to experiment and with the disposable

Juice from the 2016 harvest at Simpsons estate on the way to becoming sparkling wine. SIMPSONS WINE ESTATE

income to accept that home-produced wine will never be at bargain-basement prices.

How can that demographic be broadened? 'Try' is a crucial word: too few wine drinkers are familiar with English wine. Albury Vineyard's Nick Wenman, who has worked effectively with local Surrey publicans to bring his organic wines to broader notice, calls on more sommeliers to include English wine on their lists. More than that, they need to offer English sparkling wine by the glass. 'At £6.95 a glass rather than £40 a bottle it's much easier for people to take the plunge,' he argues.

Keen supporters of English wine already include leading restaurateurs: Raymond Blanc, Tom Kerridge and Angela Harkness are among the top chefs who

Further down the sparkling wine production line: bottling at Gusbourne. GUSBOURNE

want their diners to be able to drink wine as well as eat food whose origins lie as close as possible to their kitchens. And initiatives such as the many events during English Wine Week do a great deal to bring in new consumers.

But will there be a big enough market in the UK and further afield to absorb all the extra wine that is coming on stream, the sparkling particularly? Some in the industry are entirely optimistic, believing that, increasingly, English sparkling wine will be poured instead of champagne and other fizz. After all, the homegrown share of the booming sparkling market in the UK is still tiny. Support for homegrown products and opposition to transporting food and drink over huge distances has already massively helped the UK wine industry and should continue to do so. There will never be the sort of wine glut that some other countries suffer, but there are concerns that big increases in grape production could put pressure on prices, leading to viability problems within the industry, or open the

door to bulk buyers turning out lower-grade wine. That, says Julia Trustram Eve, marketing director of WineGB, is one reason why it is crucial that there should be a strong trade organization for English and Welsh wine.

In May 2016, Ridgeview chief operating officer Robin Langton was asked by trade magazine *The Drinks Business* how he thought sparkling wine sales would evolve in the next five to ten years. 'Honestly, it's crystal ball territory,' he replied. 'However, I hope that in ten years some of the thousands of Prosecco aficionados will finally be getting bored of this generic ambrosia and will be falling in love with ESW! At the premium end of the market, English sparkling wine will be the automatic choice of discerning consumers, quality grocers and the favourite at your special restaurant.'

That 'decade-ahead' moment has already arrived for some. 'At the moment I cannot make enough wine,' Chapel Down head winemaker Josh Donaghay-Spire

Tasting bar at The Wine Sanctuary, Chapel Down, opened in 2017. CHAPEL DOWN

Mardi Roberts: 'Together we are stronger.' AUTHOR

told me a year after Langton's prediction was published. 'We are in a position where the sales team are not selling, they are managing demand.'

In early 2017, Plumpton College's Chris Foss reckoned the growth could last perhaps a further five years. Looking beyond that, however, he was less sanguine. 'I think there will almost certainly be problems in ten years.' Others have suggested the home market's capacity may be reached even sooner. So export is crucial. The aim is to move from the 2015 base of 250,000 bottles to 2.5 million by 2020 – a quarter of likely total production.

Many of the bigger producers have progressed steadily towards achieving that. Ridgeview, for example, signed up a US-wide distributor in late 2016, when already a fifth of its production was leaving UK shores for more than a dozen different countries. Increasing both the number of bottles exported and the destinations to which they go is essential for the future of the business, says sales and marketing manager Mardi Roberts. For English drinkers, the local product is pricey and to rely on them alone would be risky. 'We won't be

Chardonnay: for sparkling wine and, in good years, still. GUSBOURNE

able to do price wars, we can't put all our eggs in one basket.' She argues for a combined effort by producers to promote exports. 'Together we are stronger, proving English sparkling wine is not a joke. There is room in the world market.'

Coates & Seely is another estate seeing, and seizing, that opportunity. In 2017 some 25 per cent of its 65,000-bottle annual production was sold to sixteen countries overseas – even reaching the legendary George V hotel in Paris. Chapel Down also counts France among its export destinations, an achievement in which head winemaker Josh Donaghay-Spire takes 'disproportionate pleasure'. Exton Park announced in May 2017 that its foreign markets had expanded to include Italy, itself a major bubbly producer. A month earlier, Waitrose headed a broad initiative to export English sparkling wines to China, selling bottles from four estates, including its own Leckford vineyard, through an e-commerce retailer similar to Amazon.

Export is the principal focus of a rather different player from the conventional grower-producers, Digby Fine English, whose wines are made from grapes sourced from contracted vineyards. 'The next twenty years will be the hard time,' co-founder Trevor Clough predicted when questioned in 2017. 'There is a lot of work to do to evangelize, to spread the word.' But export, he says, is where money is to be made.

For all in the industry the USA is a prime market, and in summer 2016 the first-ever full container load of English fizz to be exported – 5,000-plus bottles, from several producers – crossed the Atlantic. Other destinations for English wine include Canada, South Africa, Australia, Hong Kong and the UAE: in 2016 bottles were shipped to twenty-seven countries. But whether at home or abroad there is confidence that English sparkling wine will find ready sales if it remains a premium product, worthy of its price.

What of still wine? Will the improving trend continue? General feeling is that it will, with some predictions that the still/sparkling split may eventually even out. Nyetimber owner Eric Heerema doesn't agree. 'There's local demand, people are proud of serving local wines, but it will never become big,' he said in a *Wine Searcher* interview in February 2016. 'Remember also that there's an ocean of still wines in the world, and in England the yields are lower and the costs higher.' For English still wine really to take off, says Chris Foss, there would need to be the same breakthrough as sparkling has seen: international prizes, a substantial rise in production.

Stephen Skelton suggests something else could be more important: the cash reward for those who produce the wines. 'Sparkling has got a massive lead and still wine will be in a minority for years to come,' he told me. 'Having said that, if the climate continues to improve and people can sell good still wines at £15–£20, then this is so much more attractive than selling sparkling at £25–£30 that some of the production will switch.'

As for the grape varieties from which those still wines might be made, Skelton believes that climate will be the crucial factor. 'If 2016 is a marker, then chardonnay and pinot noir, plus pinot blanc and gris, become a reality. They are good because in the less ripe years they can go into sparkling and still be called "pinot". I don't see sauvignon blanc becoming mainstream, and I don't see riesling getting anywhere. Bacchus is here to stay and has enough critical mass to get known by the wine-buying public. Of course, as vineyards in the south appear to grow and prosper then people in the less favourable areas of the UK will be encouraged to try growing grapes. They will have to be growing varieties like reichensteiner, seyval, solaris, etc, because they won't get decent crops with chardonnay and pinot noir.'

Foss agrees on the potential for bacchus, pinot blanc and pinot gris. But wait a few more years, and sauvignon blanc and riesling could be joining, even overtaking, them. 'In twenty years it will be like the Loire Valley, in another twenty, like Bordeaux,' he suggested to me, speaking of grape varieties as much as of climate. And the simple message of Greyfriars owner Mike Wagstaff to growers with non-sparkling ambitions is that they should produce wines from grape varieties that are familiar to wine drinkers.

Flourishing vines at Biddenden: if the cost of English wine production is properly explained, consumers are more inclined to accept its price, says marketing manager Victoria Rose. BIDDENDEN VINEYARDS

Which points, again, to spreading the word. There is still too little knowledge about the wine made in the UK, even on home ground and especially away from London and the south. Biddenden marketing manager Victoria Rose, who hails from a long way north of Watford, admits to being one of the ignorant herself only a very short while ago. 'Before I moved to Kent four years ago,' she told me early in 2017, 'I didn't know English wine existed.' But she isn't alone in being a quick learner. 'It's incredible how far knowledge has come recently. Now it's getting to that point in Kent where not only will every restaurant and pub have it but everybody knows about it. But there is a north-south divide.'

Even for cellar door sales, Rose adds, price remains a hurdle. 'Everything comes down to the story and the time you have to explain things to people.' Low yields, climate volatility, contributing to the local economy by providing jobs for local people, the cost of planting vineyards and equipping wineries are all factors – these and more mean that UK-produced wine will never be a cheap product. But wine tourists accept that, she says, once they understand the reasons why.

Cherie Spriggs recalls that when she was appointed head winemaker at Nyetimber in 2007 she was 'shocked how few people knew about wine being made in England'. A decade later, things had changed: 'Now thankfully there is much better recognition here that we make English sparkling wine of quality that is as good as, if not sometimes better than, champagne. But we're not there yet.' Specifically, she said, more work had to be done beyond UK shores. 'Other countries still have a very poor understanding of English sparkling wine.'

Who, though, will be making those predicted millions of bottles as production continues to expand? Quite possibly not as many individually owned vineyards as exist now. Many in the UK wine industry expect some consolidation, and that has started to happen. One example was the purchase in March 2017 of Henners Vineyard in East Sussex by 44-million-bottles-a-year wine distributor Boutinot. It was the development of an existing relationship, for Boutinot had been agent for Henners since the release of its first wine in 2012, and owning an English sparkling wine company fits well in the distributor's business plan. A significant proportion of Boutinot's portfolio of wines is made in vineyards it owns round the world, in locations including France, Italy and South Africa.

Nyetimber owner Eric Heerema isn't surprised at such developments. In the 2016 *Wine Searcher* question-and-answer session he summed up his prediction for English wine thus: 'I think there will be more professional enterprises, both start-ups and also from producers consolidating with the aim of becoming more viable and sustainable. So there will be fewer and stronger producers. The biggest difference will be international awareness.'

Perish the thought that the UK might turn into solely a big-brand wine producer. But it won't, if the sensible people now making good wine continue to do the right thing. If you're a small grower and want to survive independently, 'you have to have your niche', says Albury's Nick Wenman. If you want to be successful, whatever your size, it's all about location, location, location, insists Charles Simpson: 'I cannot emphasize that enough. Site selection is the single most important success criterium.' Camel Valley's Bob Lindo believes anyone producing English wine needs to be enthusiastic about the product itself, not just its money-making potential, or they will be deterred by the lack of consistent vintages.

There are certainly ways of establishing a viable business that do not rely on coming in with a big and possibly expendable fortune. Producers such as Simpsons, Hambledon and Chapel Down have shown that successful use of crowd-funding, for example, can bring in word-spreading supporters as well as necessary cash.

One characteristic of the fledgling UK wine industry is that there has been little blatant rivalry among those working in it – other, perhaps, than at the 'one-day Olympics' held between Hampshire and Sussex vineyards. Many of the growers I spoke to went out of their way to emphasize how they worked together, organizing joint promotional initiatives, sharing information and ideas, lending equipment if a neighbour suffered a breakdown. The message to get over, they insisted, was about the quality and variety of English wine, not pushing individual producers' names. That united, friendly approach may disappear as the fastest-growing sector in UK agriculture becomes bigger and bigger, but I hope not. The all-for-one-end ethos should be cherished. As the late Mike Roberts, founder of Ridgeview, so aptly said: 'Everybody has contributed. It's what we do together that makes it work.'

The final words on the future of wine production in the UK should surely go to two people who have played a particularly important role in its present success. The first is Stephen Skelton, whose CV is impressive indeed. Skelton planted his own vineyard at Tenterden in Kent in 1977 and made wine there for twenty-two consecutive vintages. He has advised scores of would-be followers through a comprehensive consultancy service, lecturing and his books – essential reading for anyone who wants to grow wine vines successfully and profitably in the UK and other cool-climate locations. He sources and supplies vines. He gained his Master of Wine qualification with a dissertation on yeast, a fundamental element in winemaking. He has held leading positions in UK growers' organizations. He is a chairman of judges at major international wine competitions, including heading the English regional panel in the Decanter World Wine Awards.

Vines at Exton Park, one of the group of Hampshire vineyards that work together to promote their wines. EXTON PARK VINEYARD

I asked him whether, if he were to start his career in wine now, he would follow a different path. 'Not a lot different,' he replied. 'I would have made sure that I fully appreciated how much capital I needed to get established and made sure I had investors on board able to see things out for the first ten years. I would have got into direct wine sales sooner, and concentrated on tourism and visitors earlier. That way I could have sold all my wine direct. Selling wine via wholesalers and retailers hammers the margins. I would of course have started out making both still and sparkling, and started out bigger.'

And his view on the future of wine in the UK? For Skelton, the 'elephant in the room is yield and, with it, profitability'. There is a major issue, too, with continuing poor site selection among some entrants in the industry. Overall, however, his optimism far outweighs his concern. 'I wish I was 26 again and just starting out. The industry will only get bigger and bigger and with the wave of sparkling wine yet to come on to the

Julia Trustram Eve (at the Mannings Heath planting, with viticulturist Duncan McNeil): 'We are only at the very, very beginning of what are extremely exciting prospects.'
AUTHOR

Stephen Skelton (at the Domaine Evremond planting): 'The industry will only get bigger and bigger.' THOMAS ALEXANDER PHOTOGRAPHY/DOMAINE EVREMOND

market the public will be even more exposed to English wines and the demand will follow.'

The second essential figure in the success story is Julia Trustram Eve, for whom the turn of the calendar to 2018 marked twenty-five years of a leading role in promoting the wines of England and Wales. That all began when, moving out of London after marriage, she retained the wine-trade links of her earlier career by working for an English vineyard. It was a time when enthusiasm was growing among vineyard owners to co-operate to bring their wine to wider notice, and Trustram Eve was instrumental with them in establishing English Wine Producers. She became the group's marketing director – a role she retained as WineGB was established – and has prompted much of the increasing acceptance that English wine is a serious item on the world list.

She has seen and celebrated the changes over that time, and is full of optimism for what is to come. 'We have yet to see most of what is going to happen from the vines that have been planted over the last ten years,' she told me immediately after the announcement of the EWP/UKVA merger agreement in 2017. Sparkling wines will remain the main focus, with even brighter prospects as increased quantities of reserve wines become available to increase future potential. Still wines, she added, 'can only get stronger and stronger' as growers identify the best grape varieties, with 'a tremendous future' for bacchus as England's signature variety. She welcomes the prospect of more white wines from pinots blanc and gris, and reds from pinot noir, and hopes perhaps that gamay might one day join the list of English classics.

The future is bright, believes Trustram Eve: 'There are huge opportunities. We know we are producing a world-class style, and I have no doubt about the vision and focus of the sparkling wine producers. We are only at the very, very beginning of what are extremely exciting prospects.'

So there is every likelihood, not very far ahead, that the south-facing slopes of the Sussex Downs that I see from my living room window will be covered in tidy rows of vines, never a sheep in sight. I'll raise a glass of English sparkling wine to that.

CHAPEL DOWN

TOM GOLD PHOTOGRAPHY/WINEGB

A Very Brief Glossary

Biodynamic: practice of growing grapes following the rules set down by Rudolf Steiner, essentially linked to the phases of the moon and the use of composts and herbal infusions prepared according to specific recipes and applied in minimal quantities.

Blanc de blancs: white wine made only from white grapes, most frequently chardonnay.

Blanc de noirs: white wine made from red grapes, for example from pinot noir.

Chaptalization: addition of sugar to pressed grape juice to increase the alcohol level of the resulting wine.

Clones: vines originating, by cuttings, from a single vine of a specific variety and therefore having specific characteristics within those common to the variety.

Green harvesting: removal of some unripe grapes, usually at veraison, to give the remaining fruit better opportunity to ripen well.

Hectare: 10,000 square metres, 2.47 acres; an average-size football pitch is just under three-quarters of a hectare.

Hectolitre: 100 litres, approximately 22 gallons or 133 75 centilitre wine bottles.

Malolactic conversion: process changing tart malic acid (a natural component of fermented grape juice) to softer lactic acid.

NV: non-vintage, i.e. wine made from several grape harvests rather than a single year's.

Oenology: study of winemaking rather than vine-growing.

Terroir: broad term summing up the characteristics of a particular vineyard, including soil, bedrock, climate, exposition, perhaps even the grower's input.

Veraison: stage of grape development when the berries swell, soften and their skin changes colour.

Vintage: year in which a wine is made, shown on the label.

Viticulture: the practice of growing vines.

BIBLIOGRAPHY

Barty-King, Hugh, *A Tradition of English Wine*, Oxford Illustrated Press, Oxford, 1977

Brown, A.G., Meadows, I., 'Roman vineyards in Britain: finds from the Nene Valley and new research', *Antiquity*, Volume 74, Issue 285, Cambridge, September 2000

Brown, A.G., Meadows, I., Turner, S.D. & Mattingly D.J., 'Roman vineyards in Britain: stratigraphic and palynological data from Wollaston in the Nene Valley, England', *Antiquity*, Volume 75, Issue 290, Cambridge, December 2001

Gladstones, John, *Wine, Terroir and Climate Change*, Wakefield Press, South Australia, 2011

Harvey, David, *Grape Britain: A Tour of Britain's Vineyards*, Angels' Share, Glasgow, 2008

Nesbitt, A., Kemp, B., Steele, C., Lovett, A. & Dorling, S., 'Impact of recent climate change and weather variability on the viability of UK viticulture – combining weather and climate records with producers' perspectives', *Australian Journal of Grape and Wine Research*, Vol 22, 2016

Ordish, George, *The Great Wine Blight*, Sidgwick & Jackson, London, 1987

Ordish, George, *Vineyards in England and Wales*, Faber and Faber, London, 1977

Robinson, Jancis & Harding, Julia, *The Oxford Companion to Wine*, Oxford University Press, Oxford, fourth edition 2015

Robinson, Jancis, Harding, Julia & Vouillamoz, José, *Wine Grapes*, Allen Lane, UK, 2012

Skelton, Stephen, *The Wines of Britain and Ireland: A Guide to the Vineyards*, Faber & Faber, London, 2001

Skelton, Stephen, *UK Vineyards Guide*, S.P. Skelton Ltd, London, 2016

Skelton, Stephen, *Vine Varieties, Clones and Rootstocks for UK Vineyards*, S.P. Skelton Ltd, London, 2014

Skelton, Stephen, *Wine Growing in Great Britain, a complete guide to growing grapes for wine production in cool climates*, S.P. Skelton Ltd, London, 2014

Waldin, Monty, *Biodynamic Wines*, Mitchell Beazley Classic Wine Library, London, 2004

Williamson, Philip, Moore, David & Blech, Neville, *A Guide to the Wines of England & Wales*, BTL Publishing, London, 2008

INDEX

Please note that some entries, for grape varieties for example, are only the principal references.